DATE DUE

NY 27 '99			

DEMCO 38-296

THE MOTHERS OF PLAZA DE MAYO

THE MOTHERS OF PLAZA DE MAYO

(Linea Fundadora)

The Story of Renée Epelbaum
1976-1985
by

Marjorie Agosin

Translated by Janice Molloy

The Red Sea Press, Inc.
Publishers & Distributors of Third World Books
15 Industry Court
Trenton, New Jersey 08638
(609) 771-1666

RED SEA PRESS
15 INDUSTRY COURT
TRENTON, NEW JERSEY 08638

Cover Design by Duo Productions

Library of Congress Catalog Card Number: 89-63626

ISBN: 0-932415-51-2 Cloth
       0-932415-52-0 Paper

Printed and bound in Canada

Renée Epelbaum is one of the founders of the Mother of the Disappeared in Argentina. Marjorie Agosin has written a moving account of her life and the loss of her three children under the Argentinian Junta.

When you meet Renée in this book you will know that you have met majesty. Marjorie Agosin has captured the wisdom, wit and dignity of Renée. She is a person who mourns her loss without self pity and with an optimistic philosophy of life which makes our daily worries seem irrelevant and inspires us to achieve the goals of freedom, justice and humanity for which Renée stands.

Bella Abuzg

I am always surprised at the extent of "man's inhumanity to man" "raised as I was by a grandmother to believe that there is some good in everyone" I searched through the pages of this book for one single act or incident of humanity on the part of the generals and found none. Surely every human being realizes that the most painful loss to any one is the loss of a child? The most cruel act against anyone is the abduction of a loved one? Yet an entire regime demonstrated its hatred and contempt for the people of its country by indulging in the most coercive of crimes. The abduction of young people was a clear signal to everyone that the price to be paid for non-cooperation was the destruction of the "country's future". The enemies of the regime understood the message, so did their wives and their friends.

The Mothers of Plaza de Mayo is a clear and painful accounting of one nation's experience with tyranny. Every woman will feel the ache in her womb, the chill of fear in her heart as she reads Marjorie Agosin's words and thinks "Dear God, that could have been me, those disappeared could have been my children."

This time, I believe we cannot forget and we must not forgive ... that much we owe the Mothers of Plaza de Mayo.

Rosemary Brown

CONTENTS

ACKNOWLEDGEMENTS

The first time I saw Renée Epelbaum in 1985 on the program *60 Minutes*, I was affected by her presence, her energy, and in particular, her love for life — even as she was surrounded by death, torture, and lies. I became obsessed with the idea that she should one day tell her life's story. This book is the product of that dream and of a meeting with Renée that changed my life. Renée's courage, dignity, desire for justice, vitality, and love of music, life, and children are the essence and spirit of this book.

I would like to thank Renée's friend and housekeeper, Ester, for her support; my friends Osvaldo Savino and Rita Arditti, who encouraged me to take on this project; my husband, John Wiggins; and Delfina Nahuenhual, who cared for my child so that I could tell about Renée's children. Finally, I thank Janice Molloy for her devotion and the spirit with which she shaped this work. In her translations of Renée's words, she showed a true dedication to recreating her voice, her vision, and her values. Janice has lived and breathed this text and, thanks to her tireless efforts, it is possible to read Renée's story in English.

DEDICATION

To Renée Epelbaum and the memory of her three children, and to the memory of the thirty thousand Argentines abducted from 1976 to 1983 during the military dictatorship. To my son, José Daniel, and the promise of a new life.

Royalties from this book will be donated to the Mothers of Plaza de Mayo.

INTRODUCTION

Renée Epelbaum, wife, daughter, mother, and schoolteacher, never imagined the horrifying events that would almost destroy her life. On the morning of August 10, 1976 her son Luis, disappeared as he left the Medical School where he was soon to receive his degree in psychiatry. Her two younger children, Claudio and Lila, disappeared four months later, abducted by an Argentine military commando unit in Punta del Este, Uruguay, where their mother had sent them for protection.

Why did they disappear? Why did the military kidnap Lila, a twenty year old girl who had just begun to understand her own life, as she told her mother in letters? Why did they take Claudio, who always put his gloves on inside out and wanted to be a lawyer to defend political prisoners? Why did they abduct Luis, who studied medicine to cure people, and who suffered because his patients did not have enough money to buy their medication?

When I ask Renée these questions, she responds to them with a dignity filled with pain and compassion. She believes that irrationality, insanity, and greed for power are to blame for the disappearance of her three children — and nothing else.

When I began to read the extensive literature concerning the Mothers of the Plaza de Mayo, I discovered that many articles described some of these women as being sophisticated and glamorous, they were from all walks of life. The truth is that they never formed alliances with powerful people, and their power was born out of desperation and their refusal to be victims. For these reasons, I felt it was important to descend into Renée Epelbaum's everyday existence and immerse ourselves in her daily hell, and to also understand her vision of heaven.

During the month of August 1988, I made regular visits to Renée's home in Buenos Aires. Entering her apartment made me feel part of an engulfing nightmare, knowing that she had lived there with her three children, that they had grown up and played there, that they had often talked around that long, marble table. Knowing that they are no longer there. And their mother knows they were tortured and executed — but does not know how, when, where, or why.

I came to understand and feel what it is to be Renée Epelbaum, one of the most extraordinary people I have ever met. Despite the tragedies she has experienced, she can still laugh and enjoy the photographs of my son, José Daniel, which she has next to the pictures of her own children. She can still appreciate a Mozart concert in the Colón Theater, drink champagne, and toast life.

My conversations with Renée always included the question, how do you survive this unthinkable tragedy: *the loss of your children*? I also asked her: How do you get through the pain and bury those who are neither dead nor alive?

The process of getting close to Renée and her experiences was slow. We talked for hours as she showed me newspaper articles she wrote that serve as a history of the movement of the Mothers of the Plaza de Mayo since it was founded in 1976. We talked of children and of first loves. In the course of our conversations, my questions received answers that are beyond language. Renée cannot speak of her suffering because she lives that pain day after day. Still, she knows the meaning of life and what it means to be alive. Renée cannot commit suicide, although she has considered it, because then her death would be as useless as that of her children.

This book is based on conversations with Renée, Ester, her housekeeper, and me, and also on my own perceptions, reflections, and intuitions regarding the essence of Renée. The writing process consisted of extracting fragments from our conversations, words that would unmask the pain of the daily life of a survivor. The text opens with disembodied voices intertwining around a constellation of pain that opens wider and wider on each successive page. The voices are linked by something that goes beyond memory and that does not attempt to explain the human irrationality that caused this genocide.

These documents are grouped according to the paths of our

conversations. More than anything, they should be read as a conversation between two women joined by a common goal: defense of human rights and raising the world's consciousness about respect for human life.

In a letter to a mutual friend, Renée captured the tone and direction of our work:

> *I am waiting for Marjorie to arrive so we can continue our conversation. Our encounters have been just that: conversations. It is as if we were two old friends meeting again after a while and immediately retying the knot of affection and reciprocal interest. One of the topics that Marjorie and I have touched on has been the importance of putting oneself in someone else's place. We speak as if it were something natural and spontaneous. Certainly, if everyone was like this, we would understand each other better and there would be less mistrust and hostility.*

When reading this book, the reader should try to reconstruct the setting of two women talking in a city immersed in a past that has yet to be uncovered. A Buenos Aires overwhelmed by a history of terror in which each inhabitant begins to ask the question: Why did these random disappearances take place? Seeing the trials of the military officers and the former government leaders on television, every individual must examine how an illegal, unconstitutional government tortured and assassinated almost an entire generation of Argentines while the majority of citizens remained passive, not knowing or not wanting to know.

I accompanied Renée to several meetings in which students try to examine their own consciences and understand what happened in their country when they were babies. I noticed that an entire generation was missing, that of Luis, Claudio, and Lila, who would now be between 30 and 35 years old.

We spent many hours together in the warmth of Renée's

apartment in Buenos Aires, surrounded by photographs of her three children at different ages, and one of her dear husband, Raúl. I came to understand a small part of what Renée Eppelbaum feels, her sleepless nights, and her days filled with a pain that does not waver, that is endless.

How can we understand this craziness? How can we explain the genocide that occurred, not during World War II, but only a decade ago in Latin America? How can we explain the Nazi ideology and portraits of Hitler on the walls of the torture rooms?

I must recount this insanity, I must understand it from an angle that is paradoxically full of light, from a human angle. Here is the story of a survivor whom fate robbed of her three children. She survived, and her desire to go on living is in itself extraordinary.

I tell this story as an act of faith and love, as a tribute to those left behind, and in memory of those who are gone. My purpose is to make the reader of this text experience the heartbreaking pain of a mother whose three children disappeared, to feel a sense of solidarity with a woman who has survived a nightmare. Beyond all answers, beyond ideology, this book will try to speak about the absence of three children, abducted by representatives of a fascist political system, three children who cannot even be buried. The language used is poetic because I believe that only poetry is capable of expressing this horror.

Renée Epelbaum is just one of many mothers, but through her, we can understand the others. The reader will not find historical documents or statistics concerning the missing, but will find a life and will meet Luis, Claudio, and Lila, because the fight for a more just and noble society is the work of the living.

M.A.

AIDA L. BRUSCHTEIN
de SAIDON 24-12-75
ADRIAN SAIDON
24-3-76
ICTOR BRUSCHTEIN
19-5-77
NE BRUSCHTEIN
GINZBERG 11-5-77
GINZBERG
11-5-77

BACKGROUND TO A HOLOCAUST: 1976-1983

Human rights abuses in Latin America

To disappear, to cease to exist as if by a diabolical magic act was one of the most effective systems of repression under military governments in Latin America during the 1970s and '80s. Forced disappearance emerged as a method of repression in Guatemala during the 1960s.[1] In 1964, under the regime of Colonel Enrique Peralta Azurdia, 28 Guatemalan political figures and union leaders disappeared. Their bodies were reportedly thrown into the Pacific Ocean. Since then, disappearances and kidnappings have become a systematic practice designed to neutralize the political and social mobilization of citizens against repressive dictatorships.

According to figures compiled in 1985 by the Federation of the Families of the Detained/Disappeared, 90,000 people have disappeared in Latin America since 1964. 38,000 of those missing are Guatemalan; 30,000 are Argentine.[2]

The disappeared are victims who were kidnapped from their homes, their workplaces, or on public streets by unidentified armed men in civilian clothes. From the cases documented, these individuals were arbitrarily detained and taken to clandestine detention centres, where they were psychologically and physically tortured. Most were executed; others were kept alive in hidden jails under poor conditions. At times, bodies were mutilated and thrown into rivers.

The relatives of the detained and disappeared became the victims of this repressive apparatus when they frantically searched for their spouses and children. From this search sprang a number of support groups and human rights organizations; in particular, groups of mothers who defied the authoritarian, patriarchal power of the ruling dictatorships. Despite governmental decrees prohibiting these groups from meeting in public, the women defied the repressive military governments and publicly demonstrated against official terror.

The individuals in these organizations did not form part of the traditional political system; in the majority of cases, they were mothers desperately searching for their children. Women who previously did not belong to political parties were spurred into action by the repression that affected their own children and the children of other mothers.

Groups of mothers formed in Chile in 1974, in Argentina in 1976, and in El Salvador in 1981. Together these organizations constitute one of the most vigorous and original popular movements in Latin American history.[3] Paradoxically, through their traditional roles as mothers, these women have created new strategies as well as inspiration for women within Latin American politics. They are mothers who, in a society where maternity is highly valued, protest because their children were taken away by official representatives of that same society. These movements, which began as attempts by mothers to rescue their missing sons and daughters, were transformed over time into a political ideology dedicated to the defense of human rights.

Repression in Argentina

The political situation in Argentina has always been an anomaly: Argentina is a prosperous country with many natural resources, yet it has always been politically unstable. In 1930 the Argentine armed forces overthrew the democratically-elected government of Hipólito Yrigoyen of the Radical Civic Union Party. Since then, the military has overthrown five other legally-elected governments, and has ruled Argentina for longer than all the democratic governments together.

Juan Perón was a colonel who participated in the coup d'etat that overthrew President Ramón Castillo in 1943. He used his position as the head of the National Labour Department to take control of the developing trade unions, which he corrupted and used as a tool for his own personal gain. Perón became president for the first time in 1946, and was overthrown in 1955.

In 1973, Perón, who by then had become a cult figure in Argentina, returned to power. Although Perón was chosen to be president, there were many fascists in the armed forces, and they were instrumental in the creation of paramilitary groups even before the military took over. After Perón died in 1974, Isabel, his second wife, became president. However, on March 24, 1976, the military took power and the dirty war began.

The junta dismissed the congress and obsessively took on the mission of ridding the country of what it referred to as subversive thought of any kind. The armed forces dissolved all political parties, and labour unions and universities were put under government control. The junta publicly declared that these measures were taken to restore order and peace to the country.

Similar repressive measures were taken in Chile in 1973 by the Pinochet dictatorship. In both Chile and Argentina, in addition to the official actions, a subterranean rule began to take shape that used undeclared and unavowed methods of terror, repression, suspicion, torture, disappearance, and murder to put down the opposition.

At first the victims in Argentina may have been known opponents of the regime, such as labour union members, university activists, and journalists. Later, the choice of victims came to be what can only be described as random. As the crimes increased, so did the need to keep the subterranean war hidden, and attempts to obscure all traces of the horrendous acts created the need for even more atrocities. The military embarked on a kind of "final solution" with its policy of making citizens disappear in greater and greater numbers.

As unbelievable as it may seem to us now, what began as a clandestine operation became routine and bureaucratic with time. The military used teams of men dressed in civilian clothes and driving black Falcons without license plates, who entered homes and places of work at will, in broad daylight or at night, to seize and drag off people who for one reason or another were thought to be suspicious, or who were just unlucky enough to be in that place at that time. Not even children or babies were spared. Most of those seized went on to endure clandestine prisons and torture, and were later executed. The public kidnappings sowed an atmosphere of fear and terror throughout the entire population.

The years 1973-1975 saw many disappearances as well as a series of disruptive activities carried out by urban guerrillas. The actions by both sides created such a climate of mistrust and tension in the country that for some time people did not know who was responsible for the kidnappings and killings. Later, it was revealed that paramilitary groups of the extreme right, operating under the protection and authority of the military of the democratically-elected Peron, were responsible for the disappearances. It was not the urban guerrillas as the military tried to pretend.

You may be asking yourself, who were the people who disappeared? The answer is anybody who might have been perceived as opposing the regime. One did not have to act openly against the dictatorship to disappear. One could just think one's own private thoughts and still be found guilty. Statistics show that 30 percent of the disappeared were workers, 21 percent were students, 10 percent were professionals, and the rest were anyone who happened to be caught in the net, including teenagers, housewives, and even babies.

Argentina is now left to relive this painful era, to uncover what was so assiduously covered up. Where are the people who disappeared without a trace? What happened to the children snatched along with their parents? What happened to the babies that women carried in their arms as they went to the detention centres? What became of the babies born to imprisoned women? We have begun to learn the answers to some of these questions, but not to all, and justice requires an answer to all. Mothers, grandmothers, and spouses of the disappeared have been tragically forced to rescue their lost ones from the oblivion intended by the juntas, to inquire into the destiny of the almost 30,000 people who disappeared between 1973 and the return to democracy in 1984.

The world, and especially a silent Argentina, has been shaken to learn from the testimony of survivors and by subsequent excavations of unmarked graves that the disappeared were tortured and finally killed. Many were thrown into the Rio de la Plata or into the sea from helicopters. Some of the bodies recovered showed signs of death by drowning, indicating the people were still alive when they were thrown out.

Certain groups were subjected to especially sadistic treatment, especially women and Jews. Women were not arrested particularly because they were women, but *because* they were women, they were subjected to rape and other violations as well as torture. A quarter of the disappeared were women, and of those, 10 percent were pregnant at the time of their arrest.[4]

The Mothers of the Plaza de Mayo

The state of limbo in which the families of the disappeared found themselves caused them to begin a quest to find their loved ones, if only their bones. In 1975 the mothers and spouses of the disappeared started on a tortuous trek of searching. When they went to police stations or jails to inquire as to their children's whereabouts, they were often told: "It's your own fault, Señora, for raising a subversive." Or they would hear: "Your son is in the underground and is outside the country."

Because there still exists in Argentine society the legacy of Spanish culture that treats mothers with a certain respect and even veneration, the mothers were treated by police officials with superficial politeness, but were never given a straight answer to their questions.

With the guidance of leaders such as Adolfo Pérez Esquivel, the Argentine human rights activist who was awarded the Nobel Peace Prize in 1981, the mothers began to take concrete actions, such as petitioning for a writ of habeas corpus to be issued in specific cases. They still received no response to their requests.

They then asked themselves, what could they do? What

power did they actually possess? Who could have an impact in the face of such indifference? Who might have the information they sought? From this examination of the possibilities available to them was born in 1977 the group now known as the Mothers of the Plaza de Mayo. In the beginning it was not a formal organization but simply a group of women who decided to join together to protest. Their protests took place, then as now, in the same plaza where children play and feed the pigeons.

It was a strategic location for a public demonstration. Argentine independence was proclaimed here in 1810. Juan Perón gave his populist speeches here. In fact, the Plaza de Mayo is not only the heart of Buenos Aires, it is the heart of the country. The buildings that surround it include the old Cabildo, or Town Hall; the Presidential Palace, called the Casa Rosada because of its pink stone; and a number of other important government buildings and churches.

In the centre of the Plaza, there is an obelisk that commemorates the 400th anniversary of the founding of the city. Every Thursday at five o'clock in the afternoon, women begin to appear in the Plaza and circle the obelisk. Each wears a white kerchief on her head with the names of her disappeared relatives embroidered around the border, along with the dates of their disappearances. The women march in absolute silence.

The demonstrators, the Mothers of the Plaza de Mayo, are, in most cases, working-class and middle-class women, because these were the people most affected by the repression. There are some upper-class women, but they constitute a minority.

This cooperative, civic effort on the part of a handful of women without any political power, for the most part traditional housewives who had never taken part in any public action before, was the *only public protest* made for a long time against the traffickers of death in Argentina. They were the *only ones* to stand up for life.

In his book, *The Madwomen of the Plaza de Mayo*, Jean Pierre Bousquet expressed the significance of the first demonstration: "When on a Thursday of April of 1977 at five o'clock in the afternoon, fourteen women, between 40 and 70 years of age, defied the ban on public gatherings promulgated by the all-powerful military junta and marched into the Plaza de Mayo to make known their pain and their resolve not to accept having their questions go unanswered, the generals lost their first battle.''[5]

In response to the Mothers' questions, military officials used the strategy of blaming the women for having raised subversive children. They also told the women that their children were alive, had escaped from the country, and were secretly living abroad. The mothers rejected this response. This psychological tactic of creating culpability in the mothers was part of the government's strategy to immobilize the relatives of the disappeared.

During the search, the mothers suffered from a paralyzing fear of confronting the terror in which their children had been immersed, and of further repression by the death squads. Many also felt the guilt instilled by the government which blamed the mothers of the disappeared for having made a mistake in raising their children. Finally, they had to contend with the terrible psychological wound of living with the loss of a child. This reality shaped their lives, but the need to search transcended the terror imposed by a repressive government and their own feelings.

In publicly searching for their children, the mothers transformed this initial paralysis into a major force for change in the country and for rescuing their loved ones from oblivion. This step permitted the formation of the Mothers of the Plaza de Mayo, first with fourteen, then with 200 women. Obviously, the mothers who do not march have chosen silence and the acceptance of their children's death over the fight for truth.

The demonstrations every Thursday in the Plaza are now an event, a tradition, and a symbol that the Argentine people refuse to submit to fascism, but the example was started and carried on for years by a handful of women. In the beginning, soldiers would appear and simply ask them to disperse. However, as the demonstrations grew and began to have a public impact, the junta retaliated.

In 1978 the death squads kidnapped the group's first leader,

Azuzena Villaflor de Vicenti, along with eleven other members. Doña Azuzena suffered terrible tortures and martyrdom. The location of her remains is still unknown.

At about the same time, the junta also kidnapped two French nuns, whom they later gave the name of "the Flying Nuns" because they were killed by being thrown into the sea from a helicopter after being tortured. The other women kidnapped with Doña Azuzena were finally released after an international outcry, organized principally by the United Nations.

At the beginning, very few women met in the Plaza de Mayo; the original number was fourteen. Then, other women followed, and from 1976 to the present there have usually been between fifty and sixty marchers. The same mothers march, but as the years went by and people stopped being so afraid, more and more people joined them. Now, marchers may not necessarily be mothers, but people sympathetic to the cause.

The public demonstration in the Plaza is one of many activities that the Mothers are involved in. For example, they also have weekly meetings to create new strategies of protest. These strategies vary from seeking public support abroad to organizing national protest involving other human rights organizations.

The Mothers have become the heroines of Argentine society, for people realize that they were the only ones who dared to speak in a silent society. Yet they are currently in a difficult position with regard to President Alfonsín, because the Mothers, as the voice of conscience, want all the people responsible for the murders to be tried. Alfonsín has said that he will only try those who gave the orders.

At the time of this writing, the nine military officers who governed Argentina through three successive juntas have been tried in a civilian court and sentenced. The leader of the three-man junta, Videla, received a life sentence, as did Admiral Massera. Former President Viola received a seventeen-year sentence, and former President Galtieri was absolved. Three others are serving sentences ranging up to life imprisonment. Another three were exonerated.[6]

President Alfonsín has asked the Argentine Congress to pass legislation that could possible free from prosecution those officers who held the rank of lieutenant colonel or lower when the disappearances took place, as it will be "presumed" that these officers were obeying orders in a "state of coercion."[7] This amnesty would not extend to retired generals, admirals, or colonels, who seem to be the majority of those named in pending cases. The Mothers opposed the proposed legislation.[8]

The Mothers of the Plaza de Mayo continue to march because they want to know the truth about what has happened with their children's corpses. When Adolfo Pérez Esquival won the Nobel Peace Prize, it served as a public recognition of the mothers' struggles to raise the consciousness of Argentine society, and represented the acceptance of a past that had previously been silenced.

The mothers continue to create a feminine poetic imagery in their pilgrimages around the Plaza de Mayo. During these demonstrations, the Mothers wear kerchiefs embroidered with the names of their missing children. Their bound and covered hair symbolizes pain and mourning. Many women carry or attach to their bodies photographs of the missing, proving that their children existed and showing the bond between their own bodies and those of their offspring. The symbols of the kerchief and the photographs have caught the public's imagination, but there are also other acts that enlighten the world and form a link in the chain of human solidarity.

One symbolic act, at the beginning of the democratization in 1983, was the creation of silhouettes of the missing. The Mothers marched around the Plaza carrying these silhouettes. Another time, the Mothers asked observers to lie on the pavement, and they assigned each the name of a missing person. Using these symbols, the Mothers managed to personify the missing, to demonstrate that they were not just names and dates, but living, breathing human beings like everyone else.

A Swiss delegation sponsored several marches through Geneva in tribute to Argentine artists who disappeared. The participants wore identical masks representing a child, thus affirming the triumph of life over the culture of death. Another poetic expression of solidarity arrived from Holland when a group of Dutch citizens sent the Mothers outlines of their own hands, each bearing the name of a missing Argentine son or daughter.

Through their appeals to the collective memory and their tenacious presence, the Mothers attempt to recover the dead and give them a voice. The symbolism of the hands is important to the Mothers, because their hands are clean, while the hands of the death squads are covered with the blood of Argentine citizens.

FOOTNOTES

1 *For more information on disappearances in Latin America, see Amnesty International's yearly reports on human rights, as well as* Guatemala: The Group of Mutual Support, *published by America's Watch in 1985. For a historical examination of disappearances, see Disappeared: Technique of Terror, A Report for the Independent Commission on International Humanitarian Issues (London, Zed Books, 1986).*

2 *These figures were obtained from human rights organizations in the different countries, and from* Disappearances: A Workbook *(Amnesty International, London, 1983).*

3 *For more information on social movements in Chile, see the documents published by La Vicaria de la Solidaridad in Chile since 1982. Also see Ximena Bunster's article, "Women's Resistance to Pinochet and Their Struggle to Return to Democracy," in* Cultural Survival Quarterly *(Vol. 8, Number 2, Summer 1984).*

   For El Salvador, see Women of El Salvador, *published by Zed books, as well as the documents and reports of the Committee of Mothers and Monseñor Oscar Arnulfo Romero.*

4 *"Surviving Beyond Fear: Women and Torture in Latin America," by Ximena Bunster, in* Women and Change in Latin America, *edited by June Nash and Helen Saga Bergin: Garvey Publishers, Inc., South Hadley, MA, 1986.*

5 Jean-Pierre Bousquet, *Les folles de la place de Mai,* Stock 2, Paris, 1982, Page 7.

6 Shirley Christian, *"Argentine Leader Seeks to Limit Prosecution of Officers on Rights,"* New York Times, 14 May 1987, page 8, column 1.

7 *Ibid.*

8. *The most complete book on the Argentine trial was published by Amnesty International and is called,* Argentina: The Military Juntas and Human Rights (Report on the Trial of the Former Junta Members). *This book contains vital documentation concerning the beginning as well as the end of the trial from 1982 to 1985. This trial is unique in Latin American history, and represents a legal landmark in Argentina, and a victory for the Mothers.*

SANCTUARIES

When they asked her
why she was crying
whom she was looking for
she only said to them
"Return my children to me."

The light, hazy but generous, filters into the residence of these two women. Renée and Ester often seem to be guests in a house populated by the absences of Luis, Claudio, and Lila, the disappeared who are sketched behind the eyes of two women who loved them.

They survive in this eighth-floor apartment in the centre of Buenos Aires. Almost everything remains where it was when Luis, Claudio, and Lila disappeared. Renée has altered some of the rooms, but her children's clothes are still in the closets, and the letters of her dear daughter, Lila, are in a box filled with dried flower petals.

On the marble table, in the corners of the livingroom, and on top of the bookshelves are photographs of the three disappeared. These pictures affirm that they existed, that they went to high school, that they often returned to eat and converse over this marble table. Today, the photographs are constant reminders that there are three empty places at the dinner table.

There is Luis. We see him wearing a white lab coat and the dignified look of one who has dedicated his life to curing the sick. Next to his photograph is Claudio, with his tie partly loosened and all the delirium of poetry in his smile. There is Lila, with the presence of a young, restless woman who is beginning to question and explore her world.

This living room is a small sanctuary for these individuals, alive as well as dead. Perhaps some day they will ring the bell and sit down to talk with us. The photographs of the three disappeared, or the thirty thousand, peer out from the tables of this dark apartment. Where else can we go to visit them? Where are the graves where we can leave flowers? Where can we light candles for them?

Renée and Ester, the housekeeper, the perpetual guests in this empty house, looks at the pictures. I think that this space will suddenly be filled with the voices of Luis, Claudio, and Lila and the odour of innocence, because death, with its bloody sword, has not yet come for them.

This time no one knocks at the door. No one hears the children's laughter.

The women keep vigil every day and still ask themselves: *Where are they?*

RENÉE

My past is not important, although my story is as painful as that of the other Mothers of the Plaza de Mayo. To choose me or another mother will give exactly the same results, but I will tell you my story as if we were two friends talking or two friends crying.

I was born March 21, 1929, at the beginning of fall in the province of Entre Rios, Paraná. It is a very fertile area, full of hills and mountain ridges. I always picture the mountains. The landscape of my small region is curvy.

My mother was very beautiful; I don't look like her. I am plain and overweight, but one must somehow escape all this pain. They called my mother the marquise. She was like a caring yet distant queen.

I had a happy childhood. I read everything I could. When I was eight years old, I read *Don Quijote* as if it were an adventure story. This is the thing I remember most...my father's immense library. My father was a man of little education who arrived in Argentina from Odessa when he was one year old. And, of course, I remember my mother's beautiful handwriting and the scent of eucalyptus in my pockets.

I studied to be a teacher in the city of Paraná, which was the first school for teachers instituted by Sarmiento.[9] Can you imagine — he did so much for education in this country but Argentines still criticize him with that excessive nationalism for which we are infamous.

In school, I really liked foreign languages. Now I use them more than ever as I travel throughout the world denouncing the kidnappings, torture, and disappearances in Argentina and other countries in Latin America. Although they seem incompatible, I also loved chemistry and music. Now I am a businesswoman in a very masculine profession: buying and selling automobile parts.

* * *

Claudio and Lila were kidnapped November 4, 1976, in Punta del Este, Uruguay, by an Argentine commando squad. I think their names were given by other youths who couldn't control themselves and keep silent while being tortured. The soldiers asked for more and more names to kill more and more people. I think that when Lila and Claudio went to the travel agency to pick up their tickets to return to Buenos Aires for my birthday, they were kidnapped, and no one was around at two o'clock in the afternoon to witness it. The doorman of the house where the kids were staying told me they knew they were being followed, and he saw a car with an Argentine license plate following them for several days.

I went crazy trying to figure out why the death squads chose them, and the craziness of a commando unit going all the way to Uruguay to look for two teenagers.

After the children were kidnapped, I developed an infection in my retina. My eye swelled up and I couldn't cry, and you can understand how much I needed to do so. I was also speechless and couldn't scream, not even to say in the Plaza, "Where are they?" We must all fail in something.

I still can't cry now. Today — August 10 — is the anniversary of Luis's disappearance. I cannot cry and my vision is a great black wound. I wear these dark glasses to protect myself.

* * *

When we were forming a human chain outside the Organization of American States to denounce the disappearance of the children, I met a boy from Rosario there to denounce his own kidnapping. Without much hope, I asked him, "Does the name Epelbaum mean anything to you?"

"Yes," he replied, "No one knew why they had kidnapped the Epelbaums. One of them made music with his chains."[10]

* * *

During those nightmarish days, I moved as if I were sleep-walking, hopeless. Ester and I stayed up until five o'clock in the morning. The night was tremendous and lonely. We waited for the children to arrive at any moment, or a phone call from the oldest, Luisito.

* * *

I eat a lot. I have gained almost twenty kilos since the children were kidnapped. Could it be a form of self-punishment or does food relieve this pain that cuts me like a knife every day?

* * *

At home, we did not belong to any political party, but we talked a lot about human rights, especially Raúl, my husband, who died in 1965. When I saw the photographs of the other disappeared, Adela's children and the children of other mothers, I knew that they were dead, that they had been executed, because their faces were of good, noble young people. They were all so young; there were many pregnant women among them. Now, the Grandmothers of the Plaza de Mayo search for those babies.[11]

* * *

I know they never named anyone while being tortured. The proof is that many of their friends are still alive, including Adriana, who lived with Luis. My children did not speak while they were tortured. To resist, perhaps they thought of love, but I don't want to imagine what my children thought about during the torture sessions.

* * *

Everything is still intact. Claudio's books are here, and his last poems, which he wrote on a napkin. Lila's room and her vests knitted by friends. (She opens the closets and converses with her children's clothing.)

* * *

I think it is wonderful to be an adolescent, above all for their ability to be amazed and to play. Will you believe that I still have an enormous capacity to play. Even knowing that my children were tortured, I still like to joke.

FOOTNOTES

9 *Domingo Faustino Sarmiento, president of Argentina from 1868 to 1874, was a great promoter of public education.*

10 *Claudio was a musician; he played the piano and the clarinet.*

11 *The Grandmothers of the Plaza de Mayo was formed in 1982 with the establishment of a democratic government in Argentina. To the present, one book has been printed on this theme,* Botín de Guerra *(by Julio E. Nosigia, published by Tierra Firme, 1986), which presents the testimonies of the grandmothers.*

ESTER

Ester has been Renée's housekeeper and companion for seventeen years. The two care about each other and form a family anchored in memory, perhaps the only family Renée has left. Near the end of my stay, Ester offered to speak. She told me so many things that Renée couldn't say, things I couldn't or didn't know how to ask.

* * *

When Luis disappeared in 1976, the señora was crazy waiting for news, she was crazy. You can imagine how she must have felt. She always thought it was just a threat, and that Luis would reappear. For that reason, she decided not to send the other two to England, and sent them to Uruguay instead. She never realized the dimension of this horrible nightmare that had befallen us.

I always told Lila that she should be truthful with her mother about her activities. Lila was never involved in anything, but she knew that people were disappearing. She had friends who had disappeared, but never thought the same thing would happen to her.

Can you imagine what it means to disappear?

* * *

How many times did I tell the children that I wanted them alive so they could give my daughter a better future. I don't want you dead. Dead, you won't be able to help me overcome my poverty or my ignorance. Don't play with life. They said to me, "Ester, don't worry. Nothing is going to happen to us." They were so innocent and so young.

* * *

When the children disappeared, so many things changed in

our lives. Before, the señora had many friends. Those friends didn't call again to ask her to go to the movies or to go shopping, and when they saw her on the street, they blushed and crossed to the other side.

Life robbed her of her children, but I think she is still full of vitality, of desire to do things. The señora is an extraordinary human being.

We began to change some of the rooms in the house. We converted Luis's room into an office, and sold some fishing rods he had, but the rest stayed the same, especially their clothes. Everything is intact. I can't enter the children's room. I begin to say, this cannot be, this can't have happened.

To survive, I don't live in the presence of the children on a daily basis. My daughter, Verónica, lives this way, convinced she will see them again. She was five years old when they disappeared.

The señora and I talk about them at meal times and we say how much Claudio, Lila, and Luis would have liked this dessert.

When I enter the dining room, I look for three people who aren't there, whom I knew as teenagers. Suddenly, without hurricanes or earthquakes, they disappeared, and I don't know anything about them, no one knows anything.

* * *

It has been twelve years. The pain blossoms on the anniversaries of their disappearances, and I think about the señora, her bravery in living, and hope that, God willing, nothing ever happens to her.

* * *

When Claudio and Lila disappeared, the señora didn't sleep. At times, she would stay awake until six o'clock in the morning, would rest until seven, and then would get up. She frantically went from one place to another searching for information and, in particular, for lawyers who took on these things, but almost no one wanted to do it. Everything happened so quickly. She put up a shield to continue to breathe and live.

* * *

I remember when the señora travelled to Punta del Este, I prepared food for Claudio and Lila that she took with her on the plane. I prepared a delicious apple dessert. They disappeared two days later.

* * *

In the beginning, and the beginning lasted for years, I would say to the señora, "Tomorrow they will ring the bell or we will receive a letter," and we spent time chatting like that until very early in the morning and, nothing, no letter, no doorbell. The following night we would repeat the same, and the wait was so terrifying and the night so, so long and devastating.

* * *

At about three in the morning in December 1978, I heard a knock at the door. The señora wasn't home. I don't remember where she had gone; she was on a trip abroad to denounce the situation. They knocked again, and I was afraid but I thought that I should go and open the door. Ten men dressed in plain clothes stood behind the grill. They didn't have any identification, but they demanded to be let in. We climbed to the eighth floor in a frightening silence.

They searched everything, brutally. They took apart the record player, the television, the photographs. I asked them not to go into my daughter's room because she was sleeping, and she had a nervous condition and any sound could frighten her. Nevertheless, they went into her room and she woke up, yawning, making a gesture as if she were really sick.

I made sure they didn't approach her after stealing a little money she had lying around, some clothes, and the television. A young boy of about seventeen said, "Good-bye, good night, ma'am."

* * *

One day, the señora couldn't get up; it was as if she wanted to stop living. She didn't sleep, but spent the entire night in pain, lying on her bed. Then she said to me, "Ester, they have killed the children, they are not coming back."

* * *

Yes, at times I am angry, especially when one of the children's friends visits us, and I have bad thoughts and think, why them, why not the others? The señora thinks the same thing, but she never says anything.

For the señora to talk about all of this disturbs her, but she does it with commitment and an absolute dignity. It is true that she couldn't see the movie about the Mothers of the Plaza de Mayo, because her life has been so tragic, it would be as if she were seeing the life of someone else although it was really her life and she couldn't do it.[12]

* * *

Marjorie speaking: Many times, I tried to ask Renée how one mourns someone who is missing. I have come to respect those silences that are another way of talking to me, of saying what she cannot tell me, although she wants to, needs to...So I talk with Ester, the only dear and familiar person who still remains loyal, who knew and loved the children.

I ask Ester, how did the señora mourn the children? With her head bowed, she vacillates, then begins to speak.

The señora began to mourn in 1983. Finally, she didn't go

out, crazy and desperate, thinking she would find the children. She stayed in bed, exhausted, in a stupor.

I watched her and watched her and felt that she truly began to look very deep inside herself, reaching the core of her being. Once she said to me, "Ester, don't think that I'm going to commit suicide. I have to keep on living for the children."

Then she slowly began to get up and leave the depression she had created by blaming herself constantly. One day, she decided to bury the children. Now, she commemorates the days of their disappearances. Twenty days before she begins to mourn; she becomes very upset, and cannot talk or even cry.

I know the señora knows that the children are dead. I don't know what I think, but if I saw them, I would start to cry.

One morning I saw her very preoccupied and I thought she must have accepted that the children are dead. Since then, she doesn't go to the Plaza as often and she has begun to write as if she could spill out all of her pain in words.

FOOTNOTES

12 The movie, Madres de la Plaza de Mayo, directed by Susana Muñoz, is a valuable documentary that traces the history of the Mothers.

THE PLAZA

Renée speaking: In the beginning, when we would first meet in the Plaza, we were a powerless group. People laughed at us. When it rained, we looked like a bunch of heads smothered by enormous, white kerchiefs. In the beginning of 1983, with a democratic Argentine government facing a discredited military regime, we became stars because we had legitimacy in the eyes of the new government. Remember this word well, legitimacy. Our battle was legitimate; that of the military was something hidden, monstrous, and illegal.

You must also remember that, during the Falklands War (April-June 1982), we were viciously attacked. In the newspapers there were caricatures of us as horrible old women with huge knives in our backs, showing that we were traitors against the great Argentine nation.

We were the only group to oppose that war publicly, and we published numerous articles against the Falklands War. We began with the following statement: "The Mothers of the Plaza de Mayo know pain. We ask the two governments of Argentina and Great Britain to renew talks."

* * *

Too much has been said about the politization of the Mothers of the Plaza de Mayo. Politics has always interested me, but I would prefer it to be less tortuous.

I repeat that we began and continue as a movement because we are mothers; we became involved because our children disappeared. I remember that Mariá Adela (one of the founders of the Mothers of the Plaza de Mayo) went to the Plaza on April 30, 1977. She and her three sisters were there alone, completely alone. You can't imagine how afraid they were; it is almost impossible to explain because this doesn't happen in other countries. In this way, mothers began to meet in the Plaza. At first, there weren't fourteen; there were three or four. We formed strategies such as petitioning for writs of habeas corpus, because we wanted to recover the bodies or for the military to at least tell us where they were.

We were desperate, but we were also rationally searching for an immediate solution. We always thought that our children would reappear, and so we went from court to court, from police station to police station.

At three-thirty p.m. on the dot we continued to meet to share our news. I remember a particularly interesting episode. One of the first mothers of the Plaza de Mayo, Azuzena de Vicente, who later disappeared, had an audience with one of the Pope's representatives in 1976. He told us that he couldn't do much, that he had spoken with Videla and there were gray zones, as if there were some hope, gray zones...

* * *

I often thought: I don't want to be the mother of Christ. I want to be a mother who does things, who helps people, who occasionally bakes cakes, but I don't want to be the mother of Christ. For this reason, I demand that you return my son to me alive.

* * *

Ester speaking: I accompanied the Mothers when no one else would go near the Plaza. No one was with them. In those moments, I felt so helpless. Being there, not being able to do anything and knowing what had happened to the children. To think about torture, to think that all these women didn't know anything about their children and that their children had died, not through sickness or accident. They simply disappeared.

I went to the Plaza and felt that I could see their pain.

* * *

Renée speaking: One Thursday at about four-thirty in the afternoon, on my way home from the Plaza a car stopped and its occupants tried to grab me. In the car was a woman who tried to pass herself off as a French tourist, but who spoke perfect Spanish. She said, "This woman is being disorderly on a public street."

After a long struggle, I threw myself to the ground so they couldn't drag me into the car. I thought they wouldn't torture me because I was sprawled on the ground, and that's how I saved myself.

The next Thursday I returned to the Plaza, but I wore a different coat.

* * *

Ester speaking: The men were impotent when faced with the reality. The few that remained didn't want to appear in public, like at the Plaza. In addition, being the father of a disappeared person was a great stigma. Also, many of the mothers were widows like the señora, and for that reason they went alone.

* * *

Marjorie speaking: Many people greet her, I don't know how it is other Thursdays, but at least this Thursday. Distant, she smiles, telling them, I am marching, circling the Plaza for Luis, Claudio, and Lila, and also for you. A very small child watches Renée and smiles with her.

* * *

At the Plaza she wore a Cossack hat. She had watery eyes and delicate skin. She told me she was from Odessa, and that she was searching for her daughter, Graciela. Then she took off her Cossack hat to reveal a wrinkled kerchief covering her head. She said, "I am another in this Plaza," and she looked more and more like the photograph of Graciela that she carried, her eyes crazy with pain, holding her Cossack hat.

* * *

When we join arms, we form a single alliance, a single embrace, and we cross the Plaza like sleepwalkers, asking: "Where are the missing? How can we talk with them?" And a great procession of white kerchiefs blesses our innocent steps.

* * *

The crazy women of the Plaza de Mayo surround the cold obelisk. They look for their children but they know they are dead. They walk but they know there are no corpses. They walk and choose to put on masks: they stop being Renée and Adela. It is easier to be the Mothers of the Plaza de Mayo, or the crazy old women. It is easier to imagine that perhaps they will be joined with their children again, as before birth.

The crazy women of the Plaza de Mayo spin and, dizzy, we watch them ascend through the demonic air of an indifferent Buenos Aires.

The end of winter. The sun shelters us like a generous embrace. I accompany her to the Plaza. Slowly, I follow her steps and she rises as if she were an immense white kerchief watching over the ceremonies. She seems to be someone else, or am I someone else as I watch her? I see her growing and growing, and with each lap around the obelisk her steps begin to resemble the rhythms of life and death.

In the Plaza de Mayo, we are all someone else, but when the shadows fuse everything together we return to her home, and she falls silent. She is no longer a Mother of the Plaza de Mayo. She is a woman, so alone, a mother with three missing children, dead or alive.

DICTATORSHIPS

Renée speaking: This dictatorship brought pain, blood, and sweat, but it was not a holocaust merely against humans. It was a holocaust against God.

* * *

The new government has recovered the value of democracy.[13] There is a creative freedom, but one who doesn't have anything to eat cannot talk about music and art. I think the greatest crisis is the disintegration of the moral values of a large portion of the population, especially the middle class. There is a sense of desperation in the working class, which has been affected economically, because they can't even eat.

* * *

We wanted to speak with His Holiness, the Pope, for a long time. The first time the Pope came to Latin America, to Puebla in 1979, we could not see him, and when he passed in his Popemobile we tossed him a letter. The second time was in Rome in 1979, when we managed to get an audience. He listened to us for two minutes, then spoke with a soccer team for half an hour.

* * *

When Henry Kissinger was assured that Augusto Pinochet was fulfilling his duty of exterminating subversives, that is, anyone who did not share his political ideology, he advised Videla to do the same. He told him that making people disappear was good, but it had to be efficient and quick. This was published in many Argentine newspapers.[14]

* * *

The report of the National Commission on the Disappearance of People (CONADEP) published the names of many people involved with the military regime. Other names were not published openly, but it became known through official channels that one of the people who visited the concentration camps and knew the fate of the tortured was a member of the Papal delegation.[15]

Help? No one helped us. People were either accomplices or were too afraid.

We, the Mothers of the Plaza de Mayo, were candidates for the Nobel Peace Prize in 1983, but they gave it to Adolfo Pérez Esquivel.[16] You can imagine that we were very irritating for the Argentine government at that time. All in all, we were the crazy women of the Plaza de Mayo.

We founded the Mothers of the Plaza de Mayo without any political goals. We wanted to save our children from prison and torture. As time passed, we understood the hypocrisy of the government in trying to eliminate young people who advocated a more just society. Perhaps some young people promoted violence. Their methods may have been wrong, but their objectives were humane.

If these children broke the law, they should have been judged legally, and that is why the disappearances cannot be accepted. Everything clandestine is illegal. People do not choose to do something secretly unless they are ashamed, and here there was something cowardly in the air. Everything was clandestine.

In 1982, the Mothers, along with other human rights groups, began to organize something called the March of Resistance. Some friends, the same as always, accompanied us and gave us their support. Then in 1983, everything changed and we had mass support. You could tell the people were fed up. Some were angry for what had been hidden from them, and others were angry for having to keep quiet about so many horrors. I heard them shout as if they were freeing themselves. It is not enough that we are free, and now after the fall of the military government, we continue to march because the problem has not been resolved, even though we know our children are dead.

Posthumous tributes do not really interest us. Nevertheless, tributes can keep the memories alive, so we created a foundation called the "House of the Disappeared." We don't want this to be a museum, but want this foundation to go into the streets, to show movies that spark debates about the disappeared, to keep their memory alive, to support public activities. In this way, the children will always be present.

It is a mistake to believe that we can recover the past by forgetting it. It is just the opposite. We will achieve a more peaceful society by remembering, not by remaining paralyzed by the horror of the past. We must honour those who are not here.

My bitterness will not neutralize me, it will not make me negative. I try to convert my pain into a positive force in the struggle.

FOOTNOTES

13 *Renée is referring to the government of Raúl Alfonsín, inaugurated in 1983.*

14 *If anything, indeed, it is fair to assume that efforts to undermine the Carter Administration's seriousness and authority had the effect of strengthening the hand of the extremists. In June 1978, the former U.S. Secretary of State Dr. Henry Kissinger paid a five-day visit to Buenos Aires as an official guest of the regime, during which he lost no opportunity to describe Carter as a one-term president whose approach to human rights in Argentina would vanish with him. At a meeting with Argentine officials, businessmen, and journalists, each one of whom was a close supporter of the military junta, Kissinger criticized the Carter Administration for failing to recognize that it was sometimes necessary for a government to suspend civil liberties in order to overcome organized terrorism. Those countries which had not experienced terrorism might not always understand, he said, what it could do to a society and how difficult it might be to fight. "I would say that the United States owes you some understanding of the tragedies of your recent history," Dr. Kissinger said, and was applauded to the echo. Argentina was acutely conscious of money in trying to attract what it called "opinion-makers" to come to Argentina and be convinced by its arguments, and it employed the services of a New York public relations company, Bursom Marsteller, to try to combat some of the damage done by the outspoken attacks of the U.S. government. (John Simpson and Jana Bennett,* The Disappeared and the Mothers of the Plaza, *New York: St. Martin's Press, 1985, p. 273.)*

15 *The CONADEP report is one of the most basic books covering Argentina's political and legal history. This commission was created by Ernesto Sábato and the book was published under the name* Nunca más. *It was also published in English,* Never Again *(Faber and Faber, 1986).*

16 *Adolfo Pérez Esquivel was a great supporter of the Mothers of the Plaza de Mayo since the group's beginning. He continues to be one of the most important human rights lawyers in Buenos Aires.*

SURVIVORS

Renée speaking: A woman in her forties told me that she has strange nightmares every night, and that she constantly feels guilty. She is a nurse in a military hospital. She remembers there was a wing she did not have access to, but she did see women who were bad off because they had been tortured. They were brought to the hospital from the Naval Mechanics School two blocks away. The torturers brought the women to be healed so they could continue to torture them.

I listened to her without saying anything, until I finally told her that at least she has a conscience.

* * *

Osvaldo was imprisoned, gagged and isolated, for two years. When, crying, he speaks to Renée about torture, she also cries and tells him, "I have heard my three children in your voice."

* * *

A few days ago, I gave Lila's coat to Verónica. She hasn't worn it, because she told me that Lila will need it next winter.[17]

* * *

One afternoon, a friend of Luis came to see me. It had been several months since Luis had disappeared, and he said to me: Renée, I should have come to see you sooner, but a week after Luis's disappearance, they grabbed me on the street with another guy.

They kept us for a week, then released us, but first they tortured us until we couldn't bear it. While they tortured me, I wanted to die, I wanted to be dead, but when they stopped, I wanted to live, I wanted to survive.

They only asked me for names, names, and how could I

give them the names of people they would torture as they had tortured me?

When they released us, they left us with our eyes blindfolded on a main street. I couldn't walk for a month; I had sores on my feet. That is why I didn't come sooner, but I wanted to tell you what happened to me.

Now, when I'm in a bar, I hear a car's brakes squeal and I'm desperate, because I think they are coming to get me. I can't leave the country, because I don't have any money.

But I came because I dreamed about you, Renée, I dreamed that I was in danger and you were in a park and you gave me your hand.

* * *

Renée speaking: In the beginning, we thought that Isabel (another member of the Mothers of the Plaza de Mayo) had gone crazy. Don't forget that we were always accused of being crazy women, and it is certain that they will say the same about you for having come to this infamous city, for having left your seven month-old son to listen to me. Well Isabel, every Christmas she covers her table with beautiful dahlias — her daughter's name was Dalia — and she sets a place at the table for her.

* * *

Adriana, who lived with Luis for a couple of years, knocked on the door one day, crying and upset, and she said to me: "I should have marched with you in the Plaza, but I was so afraid. Now I bring you Luis."

A thin, young boy waited in the doorway. Confused, I thought it might be Luis, although he didn't look like him at all. I said to myself that perhaps torture had changed his looks and his voice. I wanted to believe it was Luisito.

Confused, Adriana and I watched him until he left, leaving us more pained and alone than ever.

The next week I learned that Adriana had been admitted to a psychiatric hospital.

* * *

Ester speaking: I always thought they would return, and we always left their favourite desserts in the refrigerator, until one day the señora told me to stop this insanity.

FOOTNOTES

17 *Verónica, Ester's daughter, is now seventeen years old.*

MEMORIES

Renée speaking: *Memory*, Marjorie, *memory*. The best way to remember the disappeared is to dedicate yourself to the struggle for human rights, to refuse to tolerate injustice or to allow them to strip us of our dignity, because when people torture, they violate human dignity. You must put yourself in someone else's skin, especially when you think of torture, which is like ripping a person's skin.

When I think of the boat people and those mothers with their starving babies, I think we should all be militants for human rights.

* * *

At times the missing are treated like paperwork. No lady, their names are not in that file, come back tomorrow. But Luis, Claudio, and Lila were not statistics, dates, or lost names. They were living human beings.

* * *

There are those who say that the disappearances should not be considered crimes against humanity because not that many people have disappeared in Latin America, they actually say that. I get deeply angered. Each life is irreplaceable, it doesn't matter if it is one life or thirty thousand. The Court of Nuremberg affirmed that each life is irreplaceable.

I am sure that if your children had disappeared, you would want the guilty to be tried.

* * *

In the fall, Buenos Aires is full of jacarandas, a fragrant flower watery with violet and rose tones. The entire city seems to be one large jacaranda. It is so beautiful to see my city full of lilies, and perhaps my Lila waits for me at home with lilies in her child-like hair.

* * *

For so many years I thought they would return from their travels. I would bring them gifts, especially to Lila. At times when I was in foreign cities denouncing what happened in Argentina, I could hear them calling on the streets. They said, "Mama."

* * *

I feel that they are always watching me, but I don't know how to look back at them.

* * *

Children who were taken with their parents form a different category: the missing who are alive. And, while we don't know what has become of them, we have every right to think they are still alive. In turn, we know that the other missing were thrown into hidden ditches, into the sea, into rivers, but as long as we don't know where there bodies are, we have the same right to feed the illusion that perhaps, perhaps...perhaps they are still alive.

* * *

Once, during a trip through Europe, we were invited to travel to Christianson, six hours from the Norwegian capital of Oslo, to tell our story.

This city had collected a lot of contributions for our cause, and the young people had gone door-to-door collecting money. When we arrived and I spoke in public, I asked how many residents lived in the city of Christianson. Sixty thousand, they answered. Then, quietly, I told them that half of the city had disappeared in Argentina.

Thirty thousand people.

LETTERS AND POEMS

Renée speaking: The military officials told us that we were bad mothers because our children had become subversives. Look at Lila's letters, Claudio's poems. Although it truly hurts me, read them to me.

* * *

Lila told me secrets and the trust between us was absolute; for this reason, I know she wasn't lying to me when she told me that she wasn't involved in political activities.

I know she told me the truth. Once she gave me a letter that wasn't sealed. Our trust was so great that it didn't matter to her, or better, she knew I wouldn't open it.

My daughter Lila was very affectionate. She left me little notes, and when she travelled, she sent me chocolate. She wasn't active in any political organization. She was seventeen-years old. She was very shy and was embarrassed about acne. I told her that she was beautiful, young, and good.

After they took her, she was alive for a few years, then they killed her. A young man told me he had met her and Claudio in prison.

* * *

I have never shown anyone Claudio's poems. They are here in this impenetrable marble table full of insomnia and martyrdom.

* * *

Marjorie speaking: I begin to read Claudio's poems. They have a sweetness and an inner energy that are full of an adolescent blossoming into manhood. How I would have liked to have spoken with Claudio, to have talked about our first loves, and of our shared love for words. But Claudio is missing; they probably tortured him for being young, Jewish, and a poet.

* * *

I found her that day with a distant look in her eyes, as if she had gone blind. Ester whispered to me that she was commemorating the anniversary of Luisito's disappearance. She wore dark glasses, and the light had gone from her eyes. She gave me some of Claudio's poems, and sounding far away and very scared she said, "This is all I have. Claudio's briefcase was burned by the neighbours in Punta del Este. They were afraid that the death squads would find my Claudio's poems."

* * *

Letters from Lila

I have recently found a new equilibrium. Although it's unstable, it is stronger than the last one.

Dear vieja:[18]
I am thinking about what it would mean for us to go, leave Buenos Aires and go to England or Germany. I don't know, all of a sudden I feel lost, as if a hurricane were passing over me. What to do?

Dear vieja:
I leave you these candies to sweeten our departure, but don't eat them all at once, spread out the doses. When you feel a little sad, eat one because they are magical candies and eating them will give you strength.
An enormous kiss.
Lila

Dear Mama:
It seems that I am becoming a philosopher. I'm not doing

too well. At night when I am alone in the garden I am filled by
an indefinable pain.

Poems by the Epelbaum children

The full moon
does not want to go
to school
but it wants to be good
what is the full moon
full of?

Luis Epelbaum, 1967

Today I observed the sky
I felt as if I were surrounded by stars.
And I thought that if I could
go to another world to talk
with its inhabitants
I could recount so many adventures
on earth.

Lila Epelbaum, 1969

Manifesto of life

First I must introduce myself,
for that is the duty of everyone
who suffers, who laughs,
for that is the duty of everyone
who writes a manifesto,
even more so if it is
a manifesto of life.

I am a life that flows
at times calm, at times nervous.

I am a desire thrown into the air,
or a desire desired.

I am who I am,
and as such
I want to enter my life,
want to be called Juan, Pedro,
or whatever.

Today, November 3, 1972,
I, with a bachelor's degree in boredom,
want to exchange my diploma.

I am nineteen years old.
I realize that at times
I don't acknowledge it
but it isn't important,
the purpose of this poetry
is to be a manifesto of life,
whether I have a B.A. in boredom
or in happiness.

I have left space to one side
and with its permission,
I am going to enter my life.

I was born nineteen years ago.
I grew up timid, crying,
then laughing, then sad,
later guilty,
powerless, wanting,
loved, loving, quiet.

I began to creep through the world,
looking to grab the bull by its horns.
After a while I stopped.

Despite everything
that happened in the world,
I, the essence of innocence,
grew up without worrying.
My brother, the one who slept
in the same house,
in the same room,
in the same world,
watched me,
played with me, gave me affection.

He was good,
good from his calm voice
to his tender look.

The only thing that bothered me
when I was born
was that I had to share
everything I had and knew
with my father, my mother, my grandparents
and all those relatives
that are with us
when we are young and spoiled.

I had to share
even my fears
that kept me from dreaming
those beautiful things
that one dreams as a child.

When I was two and one half,
another little person, a stranger,
interrupted my life.

Lila was born and with her,
the races, whining, stamping, and crawling
were reborn.

Luis and I
didn't understand anything,
who was this little person
who spent the whole day
without doing anything?
She slept, ate,
and fell back asleep.
Every day, my little sister
responsibly, rigorously,
repeated the same ritual.

I, with two and a half years
thrown into my life, lived.

When I said my first word,
everything shook.
It was like an earthquake.
Dad and Mom
hugged with joy,
Luis asked me to repeat it
I didn't understand anything.

and that is how my childhood began.

The kindergarten
where I shared my world
and where I played with my other self
that is to say with myself
although I must admit that after
a while
I tried to communicate.

At first I shared fights,
then toys,
then desires.

Every morning
I went on a streetcar,
that kind machine,
that moved from side to side
and that left me happily,
sweetly, softly,
on the threshold of innocence.

Of course, like clockwork,
at the end of every year
we went on vacation.

All of us together, all happy,
all smiles, we went to find the sun,
to throw ourselves on the sand,
to find everything
that the mechanical city hid from us.

When I entered first grade,
I was already completely a boy.
I fulfilled all the requirements
I wore short pants,
I had bangs,
and I timidly looked at my surrounding.

Then came
guitar lessons
birthday parties
school friends
teachers to whom
we declared our love in our imaginations.
Every day,
rain or shine,
we met on a corner
and played cards.

Then walking,
moving like pigeons
through a plaza,
we would stop in a pizza parlor
near our house and then,
with our smocks spotted with grease
leaving a memento of the delicious meal,
we would arrive home
dirty, without an appetite,
and fearful of a scolding by Dad and Mom
for being late.

And so, I continued to grow,
always with life in my hand,
always with my hands in life.
And so, at thirteen I reached high school,
first girlfriends, new responsibilities,
disconcerted,
clearly confused,
clearly disconcerted.

Later, my father, Dad, or old man,
whichever you prefer,
died.

I remember, it was junior year in high school.
I remember, the day before his death,
we had called the clinic
to send a doctor
(METROPOLITAN CLINIC,
SHINING CLINIC,
RESPONSIBLE CLINIC,
CLINIC WITH EXCELLENT MEDICAL ATTENTION
the ads said).

Knowing that
Dad's flu had caused the complication
of an earache,
we observed with amazement
as the doctor cautiously
asked us to call him
the next morning,
without prescribing any medication, nothing
(maybe now the feelings of hatred I have
for this non-doctor are stirring in me).
Without saying anything,
he left as he had come.
The next morning,
I remember all of this
pretty clearly,
as I went up in the elevator
returning from school,
I met the doctor from the second floor
and he told me or maybe he whispered to me,
although I assure you that his words
entered me like a dagger in my heart,
that my father, he who lived his life
with all its hiding places and roads,
was not well.
But as all human doctors,
he tried to calm
my uneasiness with death.

A few minutes later
they carried him out on a stretcher
like a sleeping child.

I still remember clearly
my mother's white, nervous,
weeping, pained, desperate,
mute face.

My sister and I stayed,
anguished, wounded,
sad, alone with the death
that hovered around
the ladder of life,
my mother mute,
my brother mute,
hand-in-hand,
the two mute ones
accompanied my father.

That night we received the news
of his death, which I had already assumed.

The house was shrouded in black,
the clothes, the hair,
the faces, all in black,
all in black.

My father went away,
with his energetic, dominant character,
with his hope and happiness,
leaving a gap in my life.

Today, three years have passed,
and when I speak of my father,
my voice still catches,
my sight still clouds over.

I must be strong,
that is what they told me,
I must live my life,
that is what I want.

Today, nineteen years have passed,
and I continue to be elbow to elbow
with life.

Today, nineteen years have passed and,
questioning what cannot be questioned,
transforming what cannot be transformed,
I want and I ask that
this small manifesto of life
become flesh and blood
for all those who read it,
this small outline of laughter
and of sadness,
of tears fallen,
of affection reserved and given,
of desire, of happiness, of memories,
and of all that is necessary to live a life,
all together for a few minutes,
in a few words,
in a few sighs,
in a smile.

Claudio, November 3, 1972

I add these timid lines
while I correct the blood spilled
in the time of the revealed truths.

I add these armored hopes
while I gather the pieces of the rose
stained by frustrated desires.

I add these tears dried by pain,
while I kiss the earth soaked
by the impotent rage
by the scandal
of the assassinated man,
his dreams lost.

Claudio, 1976

They are only some corpses
alive a couple of hours ago,
now asleep.
How I feel for you, bleeding Argentina.

They are only some hopes,
alive a couple of hours ago,
now gunned down, powerlessly asleep.
Congealed desire, atrophied happiness,
a cry scattered in a place and time.
How I feel for you, bleeding Argentina.

Claudio, 1976

She waits, she despairs...

Nine o'clock in the morning
and this cup of coffee is getting cold.
I check the clock, the woman who shares my table
reads the newspaper.

Nine fifteen in the morning,
I check the clock, which continues to tick
        without concern.
The cup empty, the ashtray filled with
        anxiety, anguish,
and cigarettes.

My daily companion smokes
while we watch the bar's glass doors.

Nine twenty-five in the morning,
I check the clock, the doors of the bar unchangeable.
Three seats, one empty.

I check the clock again,
without a word I pay for breakfast.
My companion of every morning
desperately watches the glass doors.
I am certain he isn't coming now,
he won't come, he won't come now.

Claudio, September 18, 1976

(Renée gave me this poem, saying that it meant a lot to her:)

When they gave
my son Martin
his ration of blows
they gave my son's
Jewish friend
twice as many.
When they gave
my son Martin
his portion of horror
horror isn't just that
immense fear of death
it's electricity on your testicles
and your gums raw
from the beatings.

When they gave my son
his quota of terror
they gave my son's
Jewish friend
twice as much
and this is how
the next day began.

After they assassinated my son
they felt frustrated
and they couldn't even kill
my son's Jewish friend.

More than once
let's see if
we who survive
can join hands so those who come after us
won't be assassinated
not even once
so that everyone will receive
an equal ration of life.

FOOTNOTES

18 Literally, "old lady."

RENÉE AND I: RENÉE AND US

Marjorie speaking: We laughed a lot because we wanted to experience everything in only a few days in Buenos Aires. We have such a need to celebrate life that death becomes more and more poisonous to us.

* * *

I accompany Renée to the Colón Theater. Everything is so beautiful, and someone says it is like being in Europe. There are also many concerts and marvellous orchestras in Germany. My grandfather said that the Nazis played music while they took the Jews to the gas chambers. Did the Argentine torturers play a violin concerto while they threw mutilated cadavers from helicopters? Did Mozart accompany them as they used cattle prods? Germany and Argentina, great nations of civilized people that both had terrifying holocausts.

As the indifferent inhabitants said, it must be for something, they must have taken them for some reason, or, I don't know anything about the matter.

When they took my aunt, the neighbours said they didn't know anything about the matter, but the informant lived on the floor above hers. My Aunt Stella was born and died a Jew.

In Argentina they tortured many young people, but if they were Jewish or female, they tortured them two or three times longer.

* * *

I look at Claudio and Lila's room and I think I will see them tomorrow and if not tomorrow, the day after, and I have spent all these days talking with the dead and these eleven years of hope disrupted by the horror of absence.

* * *

The Mothers mourn silently, so deep within themselves that they talk with their dead children as they walk. All of their affection, all of their love brings them closer to the image of their dead children. They seem to be inundated with memories. At times, they enjoy talking with the missing. It is as if they are suddenly filled with light, and the trees in the Plaza swell with new life.

* * *

Without doubt they are the worst victims receiving the worst punishment. They are the bearers of the most horrendous cross. They can't find their children's bodies but they know they are dead.

* * *

They parade with enormous white silhouettes. The Mothers seem to disappear behind these white cutouts without eyes, faces, or noses. They commemorate the Day of the Missing, and the silhouettes are covered with names, filled by the lives and the deaths. The city is a large, eyeless face that watches with indifference.

* * *

Then I, naive, asked her what the young people did, if they belonged to a political party or were involved in political activities. I really needed to know, to find a meaning to this insanity, although no answer could justify or legitimize these actions. So Renée, always dignified and composed, told me:

Luis was involved in a non-violent, political group called The Working Youth. They discussed ways to help in poor neighbourhoods and to promote literacy. As a doctor, he understood much of the pain suffered by others.

Claudio and Lila weren't involved in any type of political

activity. They had friends who were, but they didn't belong to a group. I will tell you that I met one of the boys who was a prisoner with Claudio and Lila. He told me Lila had said that she was also a member of The Working Youth because she had to say something.

* * *

Buenos Aires, September 10, 1988

Dear Marjorie:

I am sure that, after your return, you are resting and enjoying John's company and José Daniel's smiles. No sooner had you left than it began to rain. We had so much thunder that it was as if the sky were angry or pained because you had left. We miss you here.

The return from Ezeiza Airport to Buenos Aires was a bit difficult, and you know that no one likes to drive at night.

I'm sorry the time we had was very brief. There is a famous verse from a poem that says: *I sing my song to whomever goes with me and to be able to sing this song, to say what each of us feels, takes time.*

You tried to ask me, although it was difficult for you, how one lives and what one feels when one has experienced a tragedy like the one I have had to survive.

You will remember that I sighed. It is very difficult to avoid it. It is difficult to be a survivor because the need to live, to continue remembering, to keep alive those who are no longer with us is crucial, constant. At the same time, you always feel a great emptiness. It is almost a physical emptiness. It is as if you had a large hole in your stomach, in that imprecise area where the uterus is located, the matrix of the fetus. We notice this absence in every moment. We listen to a bolero, a song that someone sang, so many shared things. Things shared at such a high price.

It is very difficult to convince yourself that your loved ones will no longer share your anguish, and it is especially difficult when we wake up in the morning. I speak in the plural because I am sure that all the Mothers feel more or less the same way.

It is when we wake up in the morning that we cannot control our thoughts or emotions. At night, it is much easier. We go to bed exhausted, but in the morning we are invalids. We are much more vulnerable. Maybe that is why the anguish and the pain become more present. It is a tremendous blow.

When you can, write so we will know how you are.

Here we continue with a job that has been imposed on us because it must be this way. Next Monday I travel to Rosario to talk about a subject that is very important: *memory*.

Yesterday I went to hear a very interesting panel of an international meeting of Jewish writers. It was about the conflict between Palestines and Israelis and the theme of collective memory.

It is a heavy burden to make sure these tragedies do not become merely a memory, but instead are transformed into something much more serious, something of great importance. We must prevent the Holocaust and other similar holocausts from happening again.

Fortunately, news of the disappearances and kidnappings for political reasons and to foment terror has spread, and we have the obligation to keep the collective memory from forgetting.

This does not simply involve historical anecdotes. Each life is irreplaceable. We have to prevent other human beings from experiencing this pain. You and I discussed how important it is to put oneself in someone else's place.

We are fully aware that individual action alone isn't going to be fruitful, but it can help and we have to be very clear about this.

In front of me I have a photograph of you and your baby, José Daniel, just a newborn. I repeat what I have told you before about a hope I have that was part of the warm relationship I had with my children: I hope that when José Daniel is growing up, he can do so without fear, without feeling the need to crush his own dreams, without having to mutilate himself psychologically for fear of repression or for fear of incurring the wrath of those who believe they are the rulers of the world.

This morning while I was preparing the clippings, Ester told me something she forgot to say to you, of which her daughter Verónica had reminded her. During the dictatorship, we received constant telephone calls and threats, and offensive things were written on the walls of our building. Once in the middle of the night, I received a call telling me there were three tombs in Chacaritas. Three pits waiting, three open pits. I interrupted, telling the caller to jump into the pits himself, because pigs like him deserved to be there.

A big hug. I hope to see you soon and that all comes out well.

EPILOGUE

And if some were to reappear, we would have to teach them how to live again.

During my stay in Buenos Aires, I asked Renée to give me her writings, her thoughts, and her feelings. Little by little, this material fell into my hands, filled with Renée's desire to transform society and the insanity of the Argentine military dictatorship.

These writings have been grouped by the dates they were written and consist of letters sent to political figures, both national and international, newspaper columns written by Renée, and numerous unpublished documents. These documents provide a history of the movement of the Mothers of the Plaza de Mayo.

Many of these writings were published in various newspapers in Buenos Aires, especially in *El Porteño* and *Página 12*. Others are being published for the first time in this book. For some of these unpublished documents, it was impossible to pinpoint exactly when, in the period between 1983 and 1988, they were written.

1977 April 1988

We have been coming to this plaza
for ten years because

—we continue to wait for justice
—we continue to fight for life and for freedom
—we continue to say

NO to the "Final Point"
NO to "Obedience to Superiors"
NO to impunity

They are missing

> It's a pity that the ones who are missing are missing.
> We live with them,
>> for them,
>> through them,
>> after them.

> We live
>> What emptiness!
>>> How lovely it is to live!
>>> What emptiness!
>>> We walk. We breathe. We fill ourselves.
>>>> What emptiness!
>>>> The wheel turns.

* * *

Buenos Aires, April 21, 1983

TO THE INDEPENDENT JEWISH YOUTH OF LA PLATA

Dear young people:

We were truly moved by the invitation you sent us to the ceremony you are organizing to commemorate the 40th anniversary of the heroic rebellion of the Ghetto of Varsovia.[19]

The hope for a decent world, a world in which respect for human rights would be a top priority, lies in you and in all young people like you, pure of heart. You and all young people like you, who are prepared to fight for the adherence to ethical principles, give us hope that this dream will become a reality.

We want to say to you, dear friends, that we completely support this ceremony. Like you, we firmly believe that the world must not forget the rebellion of the Jews in Varsovia 40 years ago, and that we must not forget what happened and what continues to happen in Argentina during the 1970s and 1980s. The heroes of the Ghetto of Varsovia set an example for all the people of the world.

This heroic exploit in the Ghetto of Varsovia was not the first uprising by the Jewish people during their long history of rebellion against repression and injustice, and in defense of their rights and values as human beings and as a people. We recall the Macabeeans resisting to the death in Massadah in an unequal battle with the Roman usurper. We remember Moses guiding his people in the Exodus in search of the freedom denied to them by the Pharaoh in Egypt. We remember David fighting Goliath. We often think that you, us, and everyone who feels as we do fights in this difficult planet for truth, justice, and freedom as if we were small Davids fighting against an enormous Goliath with many heads. But the legitimacy of our struggle gives us strength. The force of that legitimacy is on our side, as it was on David's side.

The following are words from the Old Testament: *"For Truth toward Justice, for Justice toward Peace."* These concepts are the pillars of moral conduct on earth.

The Nazi Holocaust in Europe in the 1930s and 1940s cannot and must not be forgotten, nor should the holocaust of thousands of Argentines in contemporary Argentina be forgotten. The frailty of memory, the refusal to know, the lack of solidarity, and cowardice have allowed these tragedies to occur.

You would never allow this conduct to happen again.
We send you our affection and will be with you.

The Mothers of the Plaza de Mayo

* * *

El Porteño, December 1983

REAPPEARANCE WITH LIFE: FIRST A CRY, THEN A BANNER

The Mothers of the Plaza de Mayo is a movement that was spontaneously formed at the beginning of 1977 in response to the horrible crime of the forced disappearance of people: the kidnapping of people for political or union activities. From the beginning, we have demanded the return of our children alive.

This was our cry. Our children had been taken alive by "security forces," whose members were not charged for the crimes. We demanded that our children be set free or be publicly charged according to the law.

The official response was silence.

The armed forces carried out a true "witch hunt" in the name of "national security." They worked with a criminal mentality, that of common murderers. However, they had the power of the state at their disposal, which ensured them immunity and an apparatus that permitted them to instill terror in the country.

In accordance with this mentality, the leaders of the regime first tried to deny the facts, then tried to hide them. Later, when this proved to be impossible, they sought to avoid punishment, to be given impunity.

After a while, the truth became impossible to hide.

The fourteen mothers who formed the original group that met for the first time in the historical Plaza de Mayo on April 30, 1977, became hundreds. Their cry for the return of their children alive is now heard loudly throughout the world, and is beginning to be heard in our own country, although not as loudly because of censorship and self-censorship.

Those responsible for the orgy of crime and corruption that has descended on our country have begun to feel fear. A general stated with arrogance that "they [members of the armed forces] will never sit in the dock," but in truth his fear of confronting justice grows daily.

The criminals have used many methods to seek impunity. They even tried to force the public into silence and forgetfulness, as if this were possible! In a speech on Armed Forces Day, May 29, 1979, General Roberto Viola[20] spoke about those who had "disappeared forever," affirming that "the army regrets it . . . but will not give explanations."

For his part, General Ibérico Saint Jean, governor of the

Province of Buenos Aires, recommended that the nation forget the disappeared, saying: "it is advisable for all Argentines to throw a blanket of silence over the 'desaparecidos.'" The Mothers demand to know to which Argentines this silence is advisable, since obviously the Mothers don't want it nor is it to the benefit of Argentines. Silence is only convenient to those responsible for the disappearances.

Our cry is growing louder, our protest stronger despite the harassment we suffer.

Toward the end of 1979, the transitional government proclaimed Law 21.068, called the Presumption of Death, which shortened to only three months the legal waiting period for declaring dead a person missing during the "Dirty War." The supposed purpose of this law was to solve legal problems and ease the economic situation of the relatives of the disappeared. Nevertheless, the true intention of this legislation was evident: to exonerate the authors of these crimes.

This attempt was a complete failure, so much so that the regime itself recently repealed this law.

In the face of all these clumsy attempts to elude justice, our cry of "Reappearance with life" has become a banner. The disappeared must be returned alive, and an accounting must be given of what happened with each and every one of them.

Those responsible for these crimes must be tried.

To the immorality of the dying military regime, a regime that didn't vacillate in kidnapping thousands of defenseless people, including babies, that didn't hesitate in condemning to death thousands of young men in the irresponsible Falklands War, we, the Mothers, respond: "You took them alive, we want them back alive."

To the cowardly search for impunity, we respond: "Not forgetfulness or amnesty, return them alive."

This banner of the Mothers is not just our banner anymore, it is the banner of the Argentine people. All Argentine youth and all of the country's sane citizens, who have seen our fight as a symbol of dignity, hold our banner high. These people know that if they are silent or if they pardon this horror, they march toward their own graves. They know that we cannot forget, because memory is the only guarantee we have of learning, of ensuring truth and justice.

In this way, our original cry has become a banner and a safeguard of the honour and life of the Argentine people.

FOOTNOTES

19 *Varsovia was a Jewish ghetto in Warsaw, Poland with more than 400,000 inhabitants taken over by the Nazis in April, 1940. Despite the miserable conditions created by the Nazis and the deportation of thousands of residents to Treblinka and Auschwitz, Varsovia was the site of the most successful armed Jewish resistance against the Third Reich.*

20 *General Roberto Eduardo Viola was a member of the second military junta. He ruled Argentina for eight months in 1980 before being replaced by General Leopoldo Galtieri.*

DESPERATE CLAIM TO YOUR HOLINESS JOHN PAUL II (1984)

To the Pope of Hope

On October 28th, at Angelus time, facing St. Peter's Square, Your Holiness spoke on behalf of the "disappeared" and imprisoned without cause in Argentina and Chile.

For us, Argentine mothers, this appeal was the first hopeful light in a very long time.

Hope of truth coming to light.

Hope of charity.

Hope of justice.

In Argentina, voices can be heard today trying to minimize, to distort, to ignore your word.

The thousands of Argentines who are "disappeared" and those who are imprisoned without cause badly need Your Love.

So do we; we are lonely and alone.

They, who are agonizing in darkness, and we, who are dying in our daily "Via Crucis," beg for your help.

Dear Father, do not forsake us!

* * *

El Porteño, January 1984

THE MOTHER'S COLUMN:
WHY WE CONTINUE TO GO TO THE PLAZA

We, the Mothers, share the happiness of the vast majority of Argentines at the restoration of democracy. We participated in the general rejoicing on December 10 in celebration of the inauguration of the constitutional president, Dr. Raúl Alfonsín, although this event was inevitably tainted with mixed feelings of grief and hope.

As citizens and as mothers of the "missing and disappeared," we have participated and continue to participate in this new democracy in which the Argentine people have invested so many expectations and dreams.

This active participation implies an unconditional support of the constitutional government. All Argentines must work to prevent future coups. But this active participation also means that we must voice, publicly if necessary, our disagreement with policies or decisions that we judge to be of dubious effectiveness or to be mistaken. It is our obligation to do so, since this is the duty of all good citizens within the framework of a pluralistic and free democracy in which dissent should be expressed in a civilized manner.

To confuse critical support and the honest questioning of the methods that a constitutional government may adopt with a questioning of the legitimacy of that same government is out of the question. Firm adherence to the republican and democratic principles that mark our Constitution does not require unanimity of opinion or the concealment of dissent, since those are the characteristics of dictatorship.

It is healthy and necessary to exercise this critical support and to point out both errors and good judgement.

For this reason, we, the Mothers, will keep up our activities, without becoming involved in subordinate interests or games.

And for this reason, we continue to come to the Plaza de Mayo every Thursday. Our cry still has not been answered. The "detained and disappeared" who are alive must be released, and the government owes us the most detailed information concerning the fate of each and every one of them.

Finally, those guilty of the kidnappings, tortures, and assassinations must be tried and sentenced according to the magnitude of their crimes, the greater the responsibility, the greater the punishment. This judgement must be exemplary and known by the entire nation so it will be certain that this horror will never be repeated, that NEVER AGAIN will truly mean never again.

For this reason, we question why the accused military officers are being tried in a military court and not by an ordinary penal court like any other citizens. For this reason, we insist on the formation of a bicameral investigatory commission, since Congress, as a reflection of the general public, is the proper forum for the consideration of a problem that affects all citizens, just as the Plaza de Mayo, scene of our resistance against the dictatorship for seven long years, is the natural arena for the Mothers to continue to protest.

Only through Truth and Justice will Argentines be able to regain an ethical sense of life. Without ethics, nothing lasting, nothing that is worthwhile can be constructed.

* * *

El Porteño, June 1984

CONTRASTS

During the month of May, Buenos Aires was a scene of contrasts. On one hand, a tiny group of intolerant people carried out acts of aggression and violence in and outside of the Municipal Theatre of San Juan. On the other hand, many people offered their solidarity to the political prisoners on a two-week old hunger strike by fasting for twenty-four hours and demanding a solution to the situation.

The first episode is well-known, because it had great public repercussions, provoking general condemnation, but despite this we believe it important to mention it. Although the number of aggressors was small, it reflected a neo-fascist sector of the far right that commands great economic power and that is prepared, in order to defend its interests and privileges, since its "most sensitive nerve is in the wallet," to resort to the most tragic violence, as we have seen during the last ten years in Argentina.

We must also remember that on this occasion, the aggressors counted on police "protection." Not so the victims of the aggression, toward whom the police adopted the opposite attitude. We emphasize these peculiarities because it is necessary to be aware of the actions of these individuals dedicated to fascism so that we may neutralize them.

In marked contrast with the first episode, the second event was a beautiful gesture of human solidarity, which gives us faith in the moral and ethical values of Argentines. It reflects the same solidarity shown by the hundreds of people who gathered at the House of the Mothers, and who supported the 23 mothers who fasted for four days to call attention to our call for Truth and Justice, which still has not been satisfied.

We, the Mothers, always "talk" with our missing and detained children; they are constantly at our side and feed our strength. We evoke their generosity and their devotion to others: their peers, their brothers and sisters. This was a common characteristic to the missing and detained youth. The poem that follows, written by a 21 year old "desaparecido"[22] about policial prisoners in Argentine jails, is a living testimony of this sensitivity, of this feeling of solidarity.

> The dew falls sadly
> down your mask of happiness.
> Everyday life.
>
> In the morning the dawn greets you
> Behind your mirror feelings
> I asked you: "What is left for you?"
>
> I already see you gathering your hope,
> it is six o'clock in the morning
> a day like every day,
> collecting your bag, your food
> kissing your memories drop by drop.
>
> The sun shines, although you may not see it,
> it is certain that behind these unshakable walls
> some child kisses his mother, flesh of her flesh,
> he will walk through the same streets as always.

You will leave slowly, they will close behind you
the unknown area, terribly known
You will see the sky, the sky will envelop
   your fiery passion.
Two or three rounds, all together,
   faithful companions,
all the exercises at the same time.

The fearless walls
the hidden smiles
the never-forgotten kisses.

Everyday life.
The morning greets you.
Behind your mirror feelings
I ask you: What is left for you?

The Mothers answer this question, tinged with anguish: the message of love and tenderness for others is left for us, a message that we all must translate into action. We demand, and will continue to demand, this type of action, firmly supported on a justice that will not deceive us.

* * *

Rome, June 27, 1984

TO HIS HOLINESS, JOHN PAUL II

Holy Father:

The Mothers of the Plaza de Mayo know well, too well, bitterness in the face of injustice. We suffer from the bitterness of our children's pain as victims of a brutal, bloody repression which has been publicly denounced many times, and also denounced to you, Holy Father.

Almost seven months have passed since the end of the military dictatorship in our country, and the Mothers continue to wait and demand TRUTH AND JUSTICE. You, Holy Father, know that the Mothers do not pursue revenge, we do not demand that the kidnappers, torturers, and assassins suffer the same fate as their victims. We do ask that they be tried and that they provide the information they are retaining and hiding.

Those responsible for the horror do not show repentance or regret; on the contrary, they threaten to repeat their actions, "but this time better," in their own words.

Our newborn democracy, whose beginning the Mothers greeted with joy, will grow stronger only if we affirm two ethical principals: TRUTH AND JUSTICE.

In today's audience with His Holiness and in this note, we want to emphasize that the chaplains and priests who have been associated with the criminals and who have not shown repentance must give the appropriate authorities the information that they possess concerning the detained and disappeared. What happened with each and every one of the disappeared must be made public.

It is lamentable but necessary to mention some names: Monsignor Grasselli who — according to information from the Naval Vicariate — provided ambiguous information concerning the detained and disappeared to families that requested it. He obviously knew what was happening. The same can be said of Monsignor Antonio Plaza, archbishop of La Plata, who was seen in concentration camps by witnesses.

Other priests were also seen in these circles of hell. Their names are known. It is unacceptable that those who participated — actively or passively — in these atrocious crimes against humanity and against the dignity of humans, crimes that you, Holy Father, publicly condemned on several occasions, continue to belong to the ecclesiastical hierarchy.

We need to mention another injustice that must be corrected, involving the sanction imposed by the cardinal of Buenos Aires, Juan Carlos Aramburu, on Father Antonio Puigjané.

Father Antonio, whose own father disappeared several years ago, another victim of the repression, is a humble and exemplary servant of Christ, and as a servant of Our Father, accompanied us during the long and painful years, giving us strength in those dramatic circumstances.

He maintained our faith, which often vacillated before the cold and indifferent attitude of the highest levels of the church hierarchy in Argentina.

Father Antonio was sanctioned for having respectfully denounced this indifference and attempting to restore Christian values to people who were losing them. Cardinal Aramburu prohibited him from remaining in his diocese, the city of Buenos Aires, where he lives and where we who suffer need his Christian voice.

Holy Father, we respectfully request your intervention to revoke this decision, which is truly a scandal of injustice.

Finally, Highest Pontiff, we want to emphasize once again our anguish over the time that has passed without the achievement of the truth and justice we have been demanding in our country. Without them, we will not accomplish the peaceful coexistence you mentioned as a fundamental objective before 23 Argentine bishops on their trip to Rome last May 31.

The Mothers of the Plaza de Mayo, as well as all worthy Argentines, share this fundamental objective, which will lead to a definitive peace in Argentina, and for which we have committed ourselves without thought of the personal sacrifice it entails.

Respectfully,
Renée Epelbaum
Nora Cortiñas

* * *

El Porteño, July 1984

OPEN LETTER TO THE COUNTRY

More than seven months after the restoration of democracy in our country, the Mothers of the Plaza de Mayo believe it useful to make public our position on the current political situation and the development of the investigations of the crimes committed by the military dictatorship.

1. The Mothers and democracy

Like the vast majority of Argentines, the Mothers of the Plaza de Mayo have greeted the return to democracy with great happiness.

We are aware that this has only been possible through long years of struggle against dictatorship, during which human rights organizations played a leading role. We are equally aware that the maintenance and deepening of current freedoms will only be possible with the active participation of all democratic sectors.

The Mothers have clearly shown our desire to participate, and — despite our disagreements with certain government policies — we will be among the first to mobilize against any attempts to destabilize the democratic regime.

2. The Mothers and the crimes of the dictatorship

In his inaugural speech to the National Congress last December 10, President Alfonsín severely condemned the crimes committed by the military government. Lamentably, the instruments conceived to punish the guilty have not been sufficient for the gravity of the crimes committed.

The path chosen by the government allows the judgement of the accused by military courts, with the option of appeal to a civil court. The recent communique from the Supreme Counsel of the Armed Forces to Justice Chichizola, indicating that the notorious Astiz[23] had already been cleared by the military judge in the case of the disappearance of the Swedish youth, Dagmar Hagelin in 1977, can be taken as a sign of what might happen if military officers are tried by their peers. For a civil appeal, prosecutors must present additional evidence, in which case the military court's lack of impartiality might still determine the final verdict.

The path proposed by the Mothers consists of a double sentence — political and penal — for the crimes committed by the dictatorship.

Political condemnation involves the National Congress. To this end, we have proposed the sanction of a law that declares the forced disappearance of people as a "crime against humanity," and we continue to insist on the formation of a bicameral investigatory commission to condemn those responsible for the flagrant violations of human rights perpetrated in our country.

Penal condemnation pertains exclusively to the civil courts. We believe that the most appropriate tool is trial by jury (established in Article 102 of the National Constitution), and we support trials in ordinary, existing courts.

Our protest has a single motivation: that justice be carried out in Argentina. Our children were taken alive, and they should have been returned alive. With pain, we acknowledge that many have been murdered. With distress, we acknowledge that the possibility exists that many of the assassins will go unpunished.

For these reasons, the Mothers will continue to demand the reappearance of our children alive, because Argentines cannot resign ourselves to identifying cadavers while the assassins remain free.

For these reasons, the Mothers will continue to demand that the guilty be punished, because Argentines know that each crime that goes unpunished today may encourage thousands of crimes in the future.

We hold the profound conviction that democracy will only be strengthened by truth and justice.

FOOTNOTES

22 *Claudio Epelbaum wrote this poem.*

23 *Alfredo Astiz was a navy lieutenant who was implicated in the deaths of Dagmar Hagelin, a Swedish teenager, and two French nuns. In 1981, the military judges of the Armed Forces Supreme Court acquitted Astiz of all charges. He was then given command of a naval unit in the Malvinas/Falklands during the conflict between Argentina and England. He was later prosecuted for his role in that war and was acquitted in 1986.*

NOTES FOR THE WEEK
(1985-unpublished)

Personal responsibility, collective justice:
The official story and the trial of the members of the juntas

The Official Story marks a milestone in Argentine cinematography for a number of reasons. I want to point out the merits of this film, as indicated by the International Catholic Film Office in presenting the film with an award. The ICFO said "through current events, the movie courageously addresses the theme of personal responsibility within a collective justice."

This is the topic that I will address today and that should concern all Argentines.

Humans pass through the different stages of life, especially adolescence and youth, with greater happiness if they feel they are serving humane, ethical ideals. It is important to them that their elders uphold these ideals and live according to them.

The Argentine courts, especially those in which the military commanders of the first three military juntas are currently being tried, are now the setting where citizens (as judges and witnesses) must assume these personal responsibilities so that, within the collective justice, the people responsible for the "diabolical invention" of disappearances, to quote Cortázar, will be identified and punished.

The testimony heard so far has been so terrible and the proof so conclusive that it would be very difficult for these inhuman criminals to escape punishment. They feel trapped. Their defense attorneys and their friends argue and argue in vain to make lawful a savage and clandestine repression that didn't hesitate in resorting to aberrant methods and genocide.

What legality could there be in the kidnapping of Evelina Brull, blind and 20 years old when she was kidnapped on a public street? The "holy warriors" raped, tortured, and assassinated

Argentines, robbed homes, and stole children, even newborns.

One of the favourite arguments of the defenders of the military officers is that it is necessary to consider the causes of this "holy war" (which wasn't a war nor was it holy) and that these criminal actions were a "logical" response, although perhaps tainted by some excesses.

Among these defenders is the national deputy of the Popular Movement of Jujuy, Cristina Guzmán. This woman, a notorious friend of the "Process," especially of General Roberto Viola, who assigned her diplomatic functions although she had no experience in this area, attempted to defend the accused military officials in an article published in *La Razón* last May 21.

In this article, Mrs. Guzmán said we must "distinguish between the irregularities in a desperate battle and personal revenge; between the army and bands of men; between the misguided methods of those in command and the obedience of their subordinates. This is the sacred duty of Justice."

In this way, Mrs. Guzmán attempted to differentiate between the armed forces and commando units as if the connection between the two hadn't been documented, as if we didn't known that the bands of men responded to the orders of military officials, some of whom acted as their leaders.

The "sacred duty of Justice" is to dictate justice, and it is useless to search for excuses for the crimes of subordinates under the pretext of "obedience to superior officers." In every civilized country, individuals who steal, rape, and murder are tried and punished, regardless of whether they are wearing a uniform, regardless of their rank. In Argentina, it must be the same; the guilty must be punished.

Mrs. Guzmán also suggested that "the elaboration of scenes of horror...bury the causes under the circumstances." She does not deny that these circumstances — as she classified the bloodshed — existed. She, in addition to other right-wing politicians, also demanded that we must "respect...our institutions," including the Army, Navy, Police, and Church.

This woman ignores the fact that respect cannot come from

an order, it must be earned through actions. If the men who make up those institutions are thieves and murderers, without a sense of ethics, the institutions themselves will reflect this corruption.

OPEN LETTER TO
DR. RAÚL ALFONSÍN (1985)

Mr. President:

During your recent trip to Germany and France, you met with journalists who, reflecting the sentiments of their compatriots, asked if the fate of the "disappeared" would be thoroughly investigated and if those responsible for the kidnappings, torture, and assassinations would be prosecuted. It is obvious that in France, for example, they could not understand or accept — despite the legal explanations that have been given — that Astiz still remains free almost two years after your inauguration.

In response to the reporters' questions, you declared with visible irritation that we, the Mothers, need to prove our commitment to democracy. The Mothers of the Plaza de Mayo have said and reiterated that we are against violence; in fact, that is our credo, is what we have fought for and continue to fight for, and is explicit in our foundation's Declaration of Principles.

You are familiar with our declarations and our struggle for the return of the Constitution, so it was surprising that you said in Bonn and repeated in Paris that we need to prove that we "support democracy."

But to support democracy and reject violence does not mean we must accept the "lesser of two evils," which has apparently become an official doctrine. This theory casts shadows on the actions of the disappeared and missing, automatically converting them into terrorists. They are not here to defend themselves; their moans of pain while being tortured cannot be heard; they were not tried. To try to lessen the guilt of the homicidal military officers for the horrible crimes they committed by blaming the victims is unethical. We have not and will not accept this theory in order to prove our commitment to democracy.

We have not changed our discourse: we continue to demand that what happened to each and every one of the 'disappeared'' be revealed, and that those responsible for and those who carried out this horror be prosecuted.

The Argentine population has responded in an overwhelming fashion to the facts that have been revealed during the last several months. Almost 90 percent believe that the criminals should be tried and sentenced.

Returning to your declarations in Paris, the newspapers of September 21 [1985] printed your response to the journalist who mentioned the Mothers as "the first to fight against the dictatorship." You said: "There were many of us in Argentina, ma'am, who fought against the dictatorship and on behalf of human rights."

The Mothers never claimed to have been the only ones or the first to fight against the dictatorship, but we do claim to have been the first to have done it *publicly*, and the first to have travelled throughout the world in search of solidarity and support. Now, you are now seeking the same solidarity and support to reconstruct an impoverished Argentina that the military dictatorship left behind, that official "mafia" that trampled on the dignity of our nation and committed the most horrible crimes.

JUSTICE, HOPE, AND THE WILL OF THE PEOPLE (1985-unpublished)

Tuesday, March 12, I return to my house after a vacation. None of my children await me: Luis, Claudio, or Lila. Where can they be? What happened to them? Thousands of deaths, thousands of lives spin in my dreams — nightmares. During my vigil, I choose to remember them full of life, optimistic, with faith, lucid, dreamers, at times melancholy but always drinking in life in large gulps, generous, idealist, like so many young people I have seen in the summer walking energetically or running over the sand.

At home again: What happened, what is new? Problems with the military that seem to have been properly resolved by the government. The military's unrest is no doubt caused by the fear of those involved in the so-called "dirty war" of the progress — although slow — of justice.

Dictatorships are always intrinsically stupid, perverse, and cowardly.

The Argentine military dictatorship of the so-called "Process" fulfilled these three requirements. As an example of the first condition, it is enough to remember the prohibition against the teaching of new math in Cordoba (the domain of the "illustrious" General Luciano B. Menéndez, praised on several occasions by another "illustrious" official, Vice-President Victor Martínez. Martínez "didn't know" about the existence of the clandestine concentration camp called "La Perla," although everyone in Cordoba spoke of it, albeit quietly and with great fear).

I give in to the temptation to add another example to spur the memory and avoid our propensity toward amnesia and mention the dictatorship's censorship of certain books. In the province of Buenos Aires, General Ibérico St. Jean (another one greatly responsible for the degradation of Argentina) tried to ban *The Little Prince*[23] for being subversive!

To understand the second condition, perversity, only two

phrases are necessary: cruelty and horror to the point of nausea.

As for the third element of this trilogy, cowardice, it is worthwhile at this time, when a total amnesty is being sought for those who were responsible for the Argentine hell, to consider a few facts.

The conduct of the military authorities in ordering the repressive acts, the thousands of kidnappings, tortures, and assassinations, was both illegal and clandestine. IT WAS ALL CLANDESTINE — the detentions, the concentration camps, the executions. It was all accomplished with the greatest brutality, with the criminals hiding their faces, refusing to assume responsibility for their actions, with great *cowardice*.

Today, the conduct of those responsible is the same. Videla and Massera[25] cowardly deny having ordered illegal or criminal acts. Their subordinates, frightened by the possibility of testifying before the courts, seek immunity from prosecution. (I read today in the *Buenos Aires Herald* that *Ambito Financiero*, the newspaper that reflects the interests of the military and the juntas, reported that approximately 50 colonels recently met in the barracks of Magdalena, worried about their impending trials.) The assassins — the ones who ordered the crimes and those who committed them — should receive the appropriate and exemplary punishment, according to the severity of their crimes.

The cowards have reached the point of "every man for himself," fleeing like the cruel Suárez Mason[26], denying responsibility like Videla, Massera, and Agosti, or attempting to escape justice by threatening further violence. All this from individuals who tortured, degraded, and denigrated defenseless prisoners with aberrant practices that are against humanity and the law.

If we Argentines want to live in a decent country, if we want to recuperate our national pride, we must support Justice and prevent it from being made into a joke. We cannot accept that the notorious, cold criminal Astiz "was a victim of circumstances," as Vice-Admiral Arosa, the head of the Navy, stated.

The magistrates must set an example by taking their duties

seriously, investigating the crimes completely, and punishing severely those who ordered and those who carried out the Argentine tragedy. After his investigation, Judge Henenegildo Ventura Huayhua did not vacillate in accusing the Peruvian armed forces of assassinating eight journalists.

In Buenos Aires, Judge Julio Desiderio Burlando sentenced two police officers guilty of kidnapping and extortion (it was a second offense for one of the officers) to suspended sentences of one year six months and to only two years suspension from the force. This sentence is unusually light for such a serious crime. Could it be because the criminals were members of the police force? Chicken thieves receive stiffer sentences.

Last Saturday, March 16, Dr. Méndez Carreras, Jr. said in his weekly column in the *Buenos Aires Herald:* "There are judges who seem to be more concerned with persecuting agrarian leaders than with trying military officials suspected of the most atrocious crimes who are still very tranquilly free. The courts must always look out for the people, because justice is one of the most outstanding expressions of a civilization. Unfortunately, among us the word 'civilization' has been discredited. We must all seek the betterment of our society and avoid the dishonour of our institutions."

I believe the majority of the Argentine people have become aware of the tragedy in our country, the course of justice, and the conduct of the judges. The half a million hands that will be extended to the "disappeared" during the march on Thursday the 21st, organized by the Mothers of the Plaza de Mayo with the cooperation of other human rights groups and political parties, is proof of this.

So that young people can dream, so that we can live with dignity, I demand, and we should all demand, justice and punishment for those who violated human rights, killing our dreams.

FOOTNOTES

24 *A children's book written by French aviator Antoine de Saint Exupéry.*

25 *General Jorge R. Videla and Admiral Emilio Massera, along with Orlando Agosti, formed the first military junta, which was in power between 1976 and 1981. For their roles in the "dirty war," Videla and Massera were sentenced to life imprisonment in mid-1986.*

26 *General Carlos Guillermo Suárez Mason y Riveros, First Corps Commander, was a member of the second and third military juntas. In 1984, he escaped from Argentina after the election of Raúl Alfonsín as president, anticipating the prosecution of members of the three juntas. He was arrested in San Francisco, California, in January, 1987, but was not extradited. During the trial of the three military juntas, he was acquitted of all charges.*

NOTES FOR THE WEEK: "HOT" WEEKS, CRUCIAL WEEKS (1985-unpublished)

This is what we are living as the end of the trial of the military juntas approaches.

The question on everyone's lips is: "What will happen afterward?" Yes, we already know the nine commanders-in-chief accused in this trial will very likely be sentenced to severe sentences by the judges who make up the panel. We all assume this because of the enormity of their crimes and the conclusive testimonies. Argentines will pay attention, as will people in other countries, who will closely follow the course of the trial, the court's verdict, and the application of the sentences, so they will not be reduced.

But there remains another question related to the "avalanche of serious charges made day to day" during the trial, as Dr. Horacio Méndez Carreras, Jr. said in his article of July 27 in the morning edition of the *Buenos Aires Herald*. As Dr. Méndez Carreras also said, the government's apparent indifference in filing charges for these crimes is shocking.

In a previous note, I made the same point. I repeated a comment that had been made to me of how we who attended the hearings, with the grave accusations that were made, had the feeling that someone would run in to detain those incriminated. I also said that certainly, that was not the process that the court would follow, but instead the judges would employ other mechanisms. The judges themselves, the district attorney, and the Minister of Justice must promote these causes.

Either the initiation of new lawsuits as a result of this testimony has not been made public (and, in this case, this omission should be corrected to keep the public informed), or judicial officials simply did not act. In this last case, I would lamentably have to share the concern expressed by Méndez Carreras.

In governmental circles, no one talks about the "Final

Point" anymore. They now say that the judges will determine the extent of "obedience to superiors." Will the torturers be excused under this pretext? We wouldn't be able to believe or accept this.

Friday the ninth, retired naval lieutenant Jorge Radice, one of the alleged kidnappers of Elena Holmsberg, testified. I mention his testimony because his cynicism and shamelessness was truly astonishing. His answers altered between "I don't remember" and "I can't be sure." Questioned by the president of the court, Dr. Gil Lavedra, and District Attorney Strassera, he nevertheless admitted that he joined the group of "gangsters" within the Naval Mechanics School, working in the operative sector. His mission was "activate the weapons."

The unforgettable party

On May 23, scores of people gathered on the Plaza de Mayo to demonstrate their opposition to the government's policies. This mass of humanity gathered to protest the difficult economic situation that is gripping the nation, a crisis that is causing a recession, unemployment, and the deterioration of the standard of living for the general population, especially for working-class people, assaulted by a relentless inflation.

Although in many demonstrations of this type, certain individuals or groups try to take advantage of the situation for their own benefit, this massive gathering revealed true anguish and necessity, for which the government must urgently seek solutions...

Nevertheless, the unforgettable party to which I refer is not the gathering in the Plaza de Mayo...but rather the birthday party of Senator Julio Amoedo, celebrated in high fashion on May 23. Journalist Alberto Dearriba's account of this event was published in the May 25 edition of *La Razón*. He documented that 70 bottles of champagne, 50 bottles of wine, 6 bottles of imported whisky, etc., were consumed, as well as platters of suckling pig and other delicacies. What a contrast between the abundant food and drink at this party and the needs denounced in the Plaza.

The article also mentioned that 200 people attended the birthday party, many less than were at the Plaza. The senator has many friends!

THE ROLE OF YOUNG PEOPLE IN MODERN SOCIETY
(unpublished)

It is a fact, documented by psychologists and students of human behaviour, that humans pass through the different stages of life, especially adolescence and youth, with greater happiness if they feel that their actions reflect ethical preoccupations.

During these first stages of life, individuals feel a great need for role models and hope that their elders live in accordance with these ethical values.

A youth feels the need to transcend, not being satisfied with simply belonging to the highest level of the zoological scale. He or she feels that being human must be more than the possession of intelligence and the ability to reason, that one needs to put these abilities to the service of noble, social undertakings.

Young people then naturally fight for the rights of the oppressed, feel revolutionary fervor (in the sense of change that this word implies) and, as a natural consequence, become the opponents of oppressors who in turn, declare war on them. It is hazardous to be young, because those who attempt to perpetuate themselves through entrenched structures consider young people to be a threat to the permanence of these structures and, as such, their enemies.

This type of historical "fatality," determined in large part by the characteristics of the young soul, has caused young people to be the pioneers for the advancement of the society that surrounds them.

This role in today's society is very demanding and difficult to fulfill. Young people have been harshly persecuted by the repressive, established hierarchies for their questioning of societal values. We have recently seen this in Argentina, where young people were the principal victims of a cruel and brutal repression. Nevertheless, despite this and perhaps because of this, young people more than ever must fulfill their role, because it necessary for their development as independent human beings.

The modern world is extremely complex. Despite impressive technological and scientific advances, humans still threaten each other, motivated by an egoism and a greed that have had chilling consequences. Against this background, young people must prepare themselves with the greatest responsibility to carry out their natural roles. They must dedicate all their intelligence, will, energy, and passion to the improvement and transformation of the society in which they live, to transform it into a more humane and just environment.

Of course, this participation, this mobilization through political parties, student associations, unions, and human rights organizations presupposes an abandonment of "neutrality" and, above all, the conquering of fear. Fear is an assassin, because it transforms a person into an accomplice of assassins. Indifference, cowardice, and fear allow assassins to advance, control, and dominate.

Humans need to live in peace to be fulfilled and, although it may seem paradoxical, it is necessary for us to fight on behalf of peace in order to achieve peace. It is also necessary to live in peace with oneself, and to do so, one must fulfill the role that one's nature and spirit demand. Young people will fulfill their roles, dedicating themselves to promoting human solidarity and building a world of justice and peace. Then they will be in peace with themselves.

NOTES FOR THE WEEK
(June 21, 1985)

The Bible next to the fire

The power of the Paraguayan dictator, General (isn't it always a general?) Stroessner, was shaken by the demonstration of a single woman, Beate Klasferld, who publicly denounced the protection that the master and ruler of Paraguay bestowed upon the fugitive Nazi criminal, [Josef] Mengele.

This "demonstration" that many would assume to be irrelevant was nevertheless an important factor in Stroessner's decision to postpone his planned trip to Germany for fear of a hostile reception. It also worked as a stimulus, for shortly after, on June 5, approximately 2,000 law students went into the streets to demonstrate against the presence of the police in their study halls and in favour of freedom of expression of and the press. A protest of this type in Asunción was absolutely unexpected, given that Paraguay has been a prison-state for more than 30 years — since the beginning of the Stroessner era.

These facts confirm that an action by one person, or a few people, can bear fruit and succeed when the cause is just. The best example of this on a world-wide scale was demonstrated by Gandhi, and in our country, the public outcry initiated by fourteen mothers in the Plaza de May on April 30, 1977 against a terrorist regime.

Commemoration without fireworks

The theme of the Malvinas/Falkland Islands was treated splendidly by Carlos A. Brocato in the last issue of *Nueva Presencia*, but I must point out some aspects that have not been publicly clarified and that are important for a global understanding.

It was never publicly known that the British chancellor sent a memorandum to the Argentine government in August 1968 seeking to negotiate the return of the islands to Argentina. The Argentine Minister of Foreign Relations delayed months in responding, as if this memorandum hadn't existed or as if it had stirred little interest. The officer of the ministry was Dr. Carlos Méndez, who by coincidence was always well-dressed in English fabrics. Meanwhile, after such a prolonged period, the party that ruled Great Britain had fallen, and other interests came to predominate.

Nor has the monetary cost of the criminal affair initiated by the military dictatorship been made public. Throughout the Malvinas/Falklands affair, the dictatorship exploited popular sentiment with the transparent objective of covering up its crimes and illicit errors in public administration.

The expenses that originated from the occupation of the Malvinas/Falklands for barely two and one-half months were almost equal in per capita percentage of revenues to the expenditures of the United States during the ten years of the Vietnam War.

Nor have the Argentine people been informed that spending on military equipment during the years of the "Process" constituted approximately half of the foreign debt, surpassing twenty billion dollars. All of these figures have been published in specialized foreign publications.

Political leaders must take responsibility for this bellicose undertaking that robbed life and hope from hundreds of Argentine youth, who were thrown into a supposedly patriotic epic without being consulted, and who were poorly trained and equipped.

Today the Malvinas/Falklands, as a consequence of this delirium of the military dictatorship, has become a focus of tension and danger. To eliminate this tension and to remove the need for the British to maintain a military fortress on the islands, our government — which has repeatedly said that it will rely only on peaceful means in this area — should declare once and for all a cessation of hostilities. This would increase the chance of bilateral negotiations with Great Britain, putting our country in a better light.

We must not forget that the British are pragmatic, and that the maintenance of a military force on the Malvinas/Falklands is very costly. If the British are ready to negotiate with Spain over Gibraltar, if they have reached an accord with China regarding the fate of Hong Kong, it is very possible that an accord could be reached with regard to the Malvinas/Falklands.

Military promotions

It has been announced that the Senate will discuss this week the proposed military promotions. Some of the promotions have already been challenged by human rights organizations; among them is that of Colonel Justo Rojas Alcorta, who was publicly denounced for his anti-Semitic and fascist attitudes during the years of the "Process" by Ariel Dulevich Uzal in a letter to President Alfonsín published in *La Razón* at the end of March.

Because of this letter, Rojas Alcorta's name was withdrawn a few days later. Nevertheless, he was recently mentioned again in the local press as one of those proposed for a promotion to general. The government must investigate this situation and demand that he not be promoted if these facts about his past are confirmed.

Of judges and justice

Friday, June 14, Dr. Augusto Conte, representing human rights organizations, read a document in which he stated that numerous judges today continue to apply the values of the "Process." This list includes Federal Judge Miguel Pons, who has persecuted and ordered the detention of exiles who have returned to the country.

Of course, Pons is not the only judge who exercises his delicate task of dictating justice by applying the values that ruled during the military dictatorship... I also cite Federal Judge Nestor Blondi who refuses to release the contents of the approximately 60 voluminous notebooks taken from the study of Dr. Walter Klein a year ago. Or the Federal Judge of San Luis, Carlos

Pereyra González, who, in the best style of the "Process," invaded a student dormitory where the university leaders lived in "search for arms and ammunitions of war," based on unfounded accusations. Of course he didn't find anything. The president of the local branch of the university, Pascual Colavita, indicated that this intimidation "may make students refuse to participate and fulfill the key role that the current times demand of them."

The trial of the juntas

Day after day, evidence of chilling crimes and of the indisputable responsibility of members of the juntas continues to mount. Also, every day, it is more unquestionable that they cannot be given amnesty. This does not involve, as the usually astute columnist Pablo Giussani said in his article of Tuesday the 18th, "a punitive furor anxious to rummage through every corner of the military establishment."

Instead, we are dealing with a need for justice which is impossible to renounce because it would destroy the ethical base we need to build a free and humane society. It would imply the acceptance of living side-by-side with assassins and bestial torturers. To seek justice is not a punitive furor, it is only a need to have justice carried out.

In the same article, Giussani appealed to the armed forces to review its past with humility. I fear that he is asking the impossible, since even the government itself provided the military officers with the legal means to exonerate themselves, and we know what happened.

Important testimony was provided by Patricia Derian,[27] who clearly proved once more that the "disappearances" were a product of a system of state terrorism that was coldly planned and executed, without which the disappearances could not have happened on such a massive scale throughout Argentina. She also revealed once again the extreme perversity and hypocrisy of the military officers, members of the Supreme Court, and members of the clergy.

Pinochet once stated that he imposed a curfew in Santiago at the request of Chilean women so their husbands would be home early. The Argentine military officers, in their litany of coarse lies, told Ms. Derian that there weren't any "desaparecidos," that husbands who were not happy in their marriages went abroad. If it all wasn't so tragic, things like this would make one laugh.

Ms. Derian also reported that in 1977, the then president of the Court, Pedro Frías, said that the judges were "pained" because civil justice was unable to function. What did these judges do besides feel sad and cash their paychecks? Did they denounce the situation or protest? Where was justice?

The Argentine Parliament

The newspapers report that salaries of senators, by the decision of Vice-President Víctor Martínez, have just been raised 37 percent, when inflation in May rose "only" 23 percent. For their part, some party leaders in the House of Deputies petitioned for salaries and allowances of 970 australes, which was rejected by Dr. Pugliese, the President of the House, who offered in return "only" 858 australes for June.

We also learned that they recently could not hold a session in the House of Deputies to discuss important issues because there wasn't a quorum. It seems that the deputies are more interested in internal party affairs than in the issues that face the country.

A topic that must be discussed without delay is the Napoli Law, which would free almost all prisoners of the military dictatorship still incarcerated. It is also increasingly evident — according to what is happening in the trial of the juntas — that a commission should be formed to investigate in depth the fate of the "disappeared." What happened to all of the missing who were seen in the secret concentration camps? What investigations have taken place?

FOOTNOTES

27 *Patricia Derian was an assistant in the U.S. State Department's Office of Human Rights who focussed on pressuring the countries of the Southern Cone to eliminate the torture and assassination of political prisoners.*

NOTES FOR THE WEEK
(November 22, 1985)

The Achille Lauro and the "Final Point"

When Leon Klinhoffer, Jewish, an invalid, and a citizen of the United States, was assassinated and thrown from his wheelchair into the ocean by the hijackers of an Italian ship, the civilized world shuddered with horror and indignation. In Argentina, thousands of its citizens, mostly indefenseless youths, many barely adolescents, were kidnapped, tortured, and thrown into the ocean and rivers.

Should the assassins, toiturers, and pilots who flew the airplanes to where the bodies were thrown into the ocean be exonerated? Should they escape punishment and justice for their crimes? Should we say that "it is presumed that they acted erroneously under the legitimacy of following orders?"

This characterization was inserted into Law 23.049, Article 11 concerning reforms of the military code, to provide the criminals with a protective screen. Nevertheless, this statement cannot justify the commission of such serious crimes, unless it is presumed that those who committed them — military officers and the forces under their command — are "robots" or brainless subhumans totally without will or judgement.

And what can be said about the people who today are trying to use the "Final Point" to put an end to this tremendous story — a living, real story full of crime and pain. The "Final Point" would only absolve the victimizers, assure the criminals of a tranquil life in freedom, and make a farce out of justice. Surely those individuals are not brainless. What category then do the government officials, legislators, commanders of the armed forces, and the bishops who have demanded the "Final Point" fall into?

Some certainly belong to the category of supposed "pragmatists," for whom ethics are synonymous with utopia.

Many belong to the category of accomplices. All share a common quality: cynicism.

Recently, Representative Leopoldo Moreau (who first denounced the involvement of Battalion 601 in the pre-electoral wave of bombs and then recanted) talked with a journalist from the newspaper, *Ambito Financiero*. During this interview, he said that "the trial of one young naval officer does not guarantee the disappearance of an aberrant methodology," implying that Astiz should not be tried.

Following this line of thought, no murder should be condemned because it will not eradicate murder, nor should any burglar be sent to jail since there will continue to be robberies. The thinking of the brilliant, re-elected deputy is truly amazing!

Dr. Alfonsín himself noted during his speech on October 30 to commemorate the second anniversary of his election as president "that Argentine politicians clearly did not know how to maintain national leadership."

Although the political leadership has not been — and I fear that it still is not — of the highest quality, the Argentine people have fortunately reacted sanely and with good conscience. For example, the parents of children who are students at schools that have been threatened have organized to ensure their children's safety. They have opposed the closing of these schools, since it would imply giving in so that "cowards can become strong, can become the owners," as the text of a petition by some mothers and grandmothers stated in 1978, a text that profoundly inspired me.

* * *

Buenos Aires, June 18, 1986

To the National House of Deputies

Honorable Deputies:

Since before the end of the Military Dictatorship, the armed forces that usurped the National Government have been attempting to secure for themselves an amnesty that would protect them, along with their associates and followers, from punishment for the aberrant crimes that they committed.

Public opinion demanded that this decree be repealed.

AND IT WAS REPEALED.

Later, under two and one half years of constitutional government, the armed forces tried various methods to concede impunity to these individuals, especially through the implementation of the concept of "obedience to superiors," a protective umbrella that would let the authors of these horrible crimes go unpunished.

Ten years have passed since the beginning of the barbarity, unleashed and implemented by the military dictatorship. Many judicial cases concerning the "disappearances," the "illegal deprivation of liberty," run the risk of being dismissed. It is very worrying that those responsible for these crimes could be exonerated and remain free.

The President of the House, Dr. Juan Carlos Pugliese, said last week that 90 percent of the population rejects and repudiates the satanic methods used by the military dictatorship and condemns the atrocities it committed.

Honorable deputies, representatives of our nation, surely you share this opinion.

We come today to ask you to provide the nation with the legal means to impede the exoneration of those who, implementing a diabolical plan to benefit privileged minorities within and outside of the country, impoverished Argentina, pushed back the country's progress by decades, and committed genocide.

It is necessary to reform the penal code and introduce the term "detained-disappeared," which currently does not appear, since this crime of crimes is a recent invention.

It is also urgent to sanction a law that declares forced disappearance to be a crime against humanity. For such a crime, amnesty would not be permissible and those responsible would be subject to extradition.

We are convinced that, in this task, you will be accompanied by other groups that share the desire for justice, the only weapon we have against barbarity.

We will gladly provide you with useful materials for this bill. The O.A.S. (Organization of American States) has already declared the forced disappearance of people to be a crime against humanity, and the United Nations, through its specific body, the Group of Experts of the Subcommission on Human Rights, has recently recommended the adoption of a similar resolution.

Meanwhile, we entrust you with our hopes, the broken dreams of the "detained-disappeared," and, probably, the possibility of a bright future for Argentines.

TO BED, WITHOUT DESSERT AND WITHOUT DELAY
(1986-unpublished)

In a recent note, I spoke of the deep pain that the testimonies unfolding in the trial of the juntas[28] cause to those, like me, who have loved ones who were wrenched from their homes and who today are "disappeared." I called it the "necessary pain," because this suffering is our contribution to the causes of truth and justice, so that other mothers and children will not have to suffer in the future. We assume this commitment every morning when we awaken and say to ourselves, "Take up your cross and walk."

During the "Process," many were unaware of or chose to remain unaware of what was taking place, since the military dictatorship hid it, and fear reigned as a consequence of the system of terror that was implanted. But today, the inhabitants of Argentina *know*, we have all opened our eyes and have seen hell, a hell that took place on Argentine soil, initiated by a perverse and unscrupulous dictatorship that was motivated by greed and bastard interests and that hid its crimes behind the doctrine of national security.

Human rights organizations and individuals from different camps strongly opposed the reform bill to the military code that was passed by Parliament permitting the criminals to be judged by special military courts, by the mere action of putting on a uniform or being associated with the armed forces. This of course meant that military officers would be tried in military courts, which is against the spirit of the national constitution.

Despite our disappointment when faced with the *fait accompli*, we remained hopeful with the beginning of the trial of the juntas ordered by President Alfonsín, using his constitutional powers. We were confident that this trial would shed light on what had happened, allowing a complete, in-depth investigation that would clarify the fate of most of the detained-disappeared and, at the same time, would individualize and strongly condemn those responsible for the greatest violations to human dignity in Argentine history.

Some of this has happened. Many of the torturers and assassins have been identified by name or by easily decipherable aliases. The indignation and horror at their aberrant crimes is so great that a few days ago, a foreign journalist who has attended the trials said that when he heard some of the testimony, he kept waiting for someone to run out to detain the criminals. Of course, this is just a figure of speech, but he was expressing a general feeling, since the wheels of justice turn much more slowly.

Nevertheless, despite this horror that we are living and reliving day after day, officials close to the president have recently said that certain individuals were working on an amnesty bill. This amnesty will probably be disguised under another name, perhaps that of the "Final Point," or will be carried out through a legal sleight-of-hand, such as a new amendment to the military code that would give impunity to almost everyone involved in these crimes against humanity under the guise of "following orders from superiors."

The attempts to justify this amnesty are completely invalid. For example, in a recent radio interview, the president of the House of Deputies, Dr. Juan Carlos Pugliese, recently claimed that the country "needs to look forward, leaving the past behind as soon as possible." HOWEVER, A NATION THAT DOESN'T HAVE A MEMORY DOESN'T HAVE A FUTURE. Such a country will fatefully repeat the same actions, even though they may lead to its destruction.

On July 1, President Raúl Alfonsín sent a message to the Permanent Assembly of Human Rights in celebration of that institution's tenth anniversary. I will quote two passages from his message, with which all Argentines are familiar. The president stated that we must maintain a "cautious vigil in the face of violence and authoritarianism to reconstruct human dignity and form the basis of a participatory, democratic society, free from the fears, tortures, and humiliations that darkened the

Argentine sky." He added: "The people and the government must work together to defeat definitively any lapses and to achieve a final reconciliation according to a permanent and invulnerable set of ethical standards."

We who denounce the attempt to concede impunity to criminals share that "cautious vigil" and reject an amnesty that pushes aside the ethical bases that Dr. Alfonsín favored in his message.

To exonerate those responsible for this great crime that covered our country in blood, tears, and pain is to undermine our constitutional, democratic system and encourages its enemies to revive their attempts to usurp political power.

It is also necessary to make an important point: an amnesty, whatever it is called or however it is implemented, closes forever all investigations taking place regarding the fate of the detained-disappeared, which is precisely what those responsible for the crimes want. This would constitute a concealment of the truth, the institutionalization of injustice, not justice.

If most of the "violators of humankind," the torturers, and the assassins are exonerated and only a small group of military officers pays for the crimes, in a way that can be seen as being light in relation to the magnitude of their crimes (it would be as if a naughty child's parent sent him to bed without dinner), if the people who today hold government posts assume the responsibility and the consequences of this type of decision, skepticism and lack of faith will undoubtedly become an integral part of the spiritual baggage of all Argentines. A truly grim prospect...I hope there is still room for reflection.

* * *

September 21, 1987

OPEN LETTER TO THE PEOPLE

September 21 is the first day of spring, the day of young people and of hope for a better tomorrow.

September 21 is a day of happiness for those who are here,

and a day of pain for those who are not here, those who cannot celebrate today because yesterday they were kidnapped for being young, generous, and compassionate.

Young people will continue to flourish, full of dreams, passionate, stubborn, and searching for love and justice, for this is what it means to be young.

We hope this September 21 will be a bright day for all of Argentina's youths.

The Founders of the Mothers of the Plaza de Mayo

* * *

Página 12, October 7, 1987

THE BEST TRIBUTE

Empty landscapes

The two first weeks of December are filled with remembrances, tributes, and celebrations. Next December 10 will mark the 39th anniversary of the Universal Declaration of Human Rights and, in our country, the fourth anniversary of the reestablishment of a constitutional government. Throughout Argentina's history, this is an occasion that we seldom have had the chance to celebrate.

Of course, although the return to democracy is important, it is not enough. Most Argentines, so hopeful at the beginning, now feel cheated by a government that has proven to be weak and complaisant with the military and that has not been able to respond to the needs and pain of the large sector of the population living in poverty.

Nevertheless, this transitional government (as many different groups refer to it) allows what no dictatorship, and few constitutional governments, would ever tolerate: a freedom of expression that allows dissent and open discussion of problems.

So we celebrate these four years and all of us light another candle with our daily actions, demanding that those with decision-making power fulfill their duties for the benefit of the country and for *all citizens*, since by definition, a country is its people, who work and dream, experience happiness and suffering. Without its people, a country is only empty landscapes.

Universal Declaration of Human Rights

This anniversary finds Argentines in a moment of great conflict. The laws of the "Final Point" and "Obedience to Superiors" have provided pardons and a way of escape for most of the criminals who, as members and servants of state terrorism, kidnapped, tortured, assassinated, and plundered their victims and the country.

The escalating anti-Semitism in our country is in part a consequence of this impunity. The corruption and criminality of police groups revealed by the actions of two honest judges, Dr. Irurzun and Dr. Ramos Padilla, rare birds within a discredited judiciary, is a sad reflection on our country.

An example of this is Taddei, known as "The Priest," who participated in the kidnapping of Osvaldo Sivak. Taddei, a former police officer and member of Battalion 601 of the security forces, is now a fugitive and presumably living in Europe and enjoying freedom and fortune. The few survivors of the El Banco Concentration Camp, run by then Mayor Minicucci, now promoted by the current government to Lieutenant Colonel, have recognized Taddei as one of the two principal kidnappers and torturers. The other was Juan A. del Cerro, known as "Colors."

The thousands of young Jews and gentiles, the generation that is missing today and whose loss mutilated our society, could now be serving their communities and the country. They were kidnapped for being thinkers, for being sensitive to the challenges that face our society. To understand their concerns, one must simply go into one of our city's slums. The only ones who, wouldn't see the despair would be those who didn't want to see and shut their eyes and their hearts.

Remembrances and tributes

From December 3 to 11 there will be various events dedicated to those kidnapped between December 8 and 10, 1977. On December 9, 1977, thirteen friends and relatives of the missing and two French nuns who tried to collect money to publish an ad demanding justice for the "desaparecidos" were kidnapped from the Santa Cruz de María Church. Among those who were kidnapped were three mothers, including Azuzena Villaflor de De Vicenti, who founded the movement of the Mothers of the Plaza de Mayo. All of them became "desaparecidos."

This story, including the participation of then Lieutenant Astiz, who is still in active service and about to be promoted to captain, is well-known, so I will not go into detail. Also widely acknowledged is the obstinacy of the mothers and relatives of the victims and those who gave their support in demanding the reappearance of those who had been kidnapped. These individuals later pressured the government for a thorough investigation to determine what had become of the missing, a demand that can be summed up in two words: truth and justice.

But what cannot be verbalized is the suffering, the pain behind this demand.

During the years of the military dictatorship, the biblical "Love others as you love yourself" was absent. Hatred, scorn for others, humiliation of human beings, and violation of the dignity of the body and soul ruled.

We must eliminate this type of conduct forever. It is essential to reevaluate ethics, morality, and justice. The French philosopher Jankelvitch said in reference to the Holocaust: "It is necessary to invert the phrase of the Gospel and say instead 'Father do not forgive them because they know what they are doing.'" The best tribute we can offer the victims of state terrorism in Argentina is not to forget, is to demand justice.

LETTERS

To Poema Ackerman

I have wanted to write to you since September 22 when, in the morgue, they gave you the remains of your daughter, Leticia, "in a small box covered with black cloth." I wasn't able to accompany you, but I would have liked to have said many things to you... That is why I am writing today.

The previous day thousands of young people celebrated the first day of spring, but Leticia, so young, only 18 years old when she was kidnapped in April 1976, couldn't share the joyful festivities. Cowardly assassins had gunned down her dreams and her laughter, in July 1976, three months after she was kidnapped. These criminals are still loose; they walk around in freedom, and may never be tried or sentenced, thanks to the laws of the "Final Point" and "Orders from Superiors," a moral and legal monstrosity destined to help monsters like Leticia's kidnappers and murderers.

Yesterday was the Day of Atonement, which the Jewish community consecrates as our most important holiday. Believers and non-believers reflect in the week that follows the festivities of Rosh Hashana, the Jewish New Year. After this examination of one's conscience, one prays for forgiveness for injustices committed and for the lack of charity. Did Leticia's assassins ever reflect like this? Did they ask for forgiveness? I doubt it...

Her assassins seek honours and forgetfulness. But they will not have it. As long as you live, Leticia will be alive in you, and Leticia's friends and everyone she loved and who loved her will remember her. Leticia will live. And above all, she will live in other Leticias who are blossoming and will continue to blossom, who will not have exactly the same smile as your Leticia, but they will be smiles made from the same dreams and desires. As long as this is true, there will still be room for hope.

* * *

December 5, 1987

Buenos Aires, January 8, 1988

Dr. Dante Caputo
Minister of Foreign Relations

Dear Chancellor:

Delegates of eight Latin American governments are currently travelling through Central America, verifying the fulfillment of the Accords of Esquipulas II according to the procedures established by those Accords.

The signature of the Accords of Esquipulas II signified the possibility of achieving peace in that region of our continent that has been so torn by years of war and by the constant violation of the most basic human rights.

The presentation of the Nobel Peace Prize to the president of Costa Rica, Oscar Arias, initiator of those Accords, was recognition of this hope for peace.

The 15th of this month, there will be a meeting in Costa Rica to examine the results of this verification trip. Without doubt, the desired results have not yet been achieved, in large part due to the strong opposition of the Reagan Administration, which is sabotaging these Accords by supporting the Contras.

Nevertheless, these steps toward peace must continue to be supported and take root. This is the only possible way to avoid a full-scale war, with its accompanying blood and horror.

Argentina, a member of the Contadora Support Group whose influence in Latin America was felt during the last meeting in Acapulco, has an important role in these efforts for peace.

We ask you, Dr. Caputo, to make the voice of our country heard during the meeting on the 15th, promoting the extension of the peace process and strengthening it, and requiring the cessation of support for the Contras, an obvious source of unrest in the region.

Sincerely,

Renée S. de Epelbaum
Carmen Lapacó

* * *

Buenos Aires, February 16, 1988

Commission on Human Rights
Office of the United Nations in Geneva
Bureau D-107
1211 Geneva 10
Switzerland

There exists a world-wide consensus that the "forced disappearance of people" constitutes the crime of crimes, since it includes all other crimes: kidnapping, torture, rape, and murder. Thus, it is urgent that this Commission propose to the United Nations General Assembly a resolution characterizing this offense as a crime against humanity. This resolution will not only be a tool in punishing the guilty, but also will serve as a deterrent.

At the same time, we call your attention to two laws enacted by the Argentine government in December 1986 and May 1987, numbers 23.492 and 23.521 respectively, known as the "Final Point" and "Obedience to Superiors." These laws contradict the National Constitution and international accords by constituting a privation of justice by establishing a virtual amnesty for those who committed crimes against humanity during the state terrorism instituted by the Argentine military dictatorship.

We trust that the Commission will take our request into account.

Buenos Aires, May 11, 1988

To the President of the Supreme Court of Justice, Dr. José Severo Caballero, and the Judges of the Supreme Court, Dr. Jorge A. Bacqué, Dr. Augusto Belluscio, Dr. Carlos Fayt, and Dr. Enrique Petracchi

Honorable Judges:

History records famous verdicts that, for their ethical content, become examples. The judges who give these opinions become universal models.

Such is the case of the judges of the Nuremberg Trial, who refused to accept "obedience to superiors" as a justification or extenuating circumstance for the Nazi crimes against humanity.

The same spirit guided the Israeli judge, Zvi Tal, who in recently condemning Demjanjuk — called Ivan the Terrible by the victims of his sadism in Treblinka — said that his crimes were of the type that can never be pardoned, "NOT BY THE LETTER OF THE LAW NOR IN THE HEARTS OF THE PEOPLE."

The crimes committed during the military regime implanted in our country by the coup of March 1976 belong to this same category.

Nevertheless, with astonishment, we have seen the High Court validate laws that are clearly unconstitutional, laws that pardon these crimes. We are obviously referring to the laws known as the "Final Point" and "Obedience to Superiors."

Previously, and with equal outrage, we saw how Attorney General Dr. Andrés D'Alessio and Assistant Prosecutor Dr. Jaime Malamud Gotti solicited the dismissal of charges against many of the military officers involved in the commission of these crimes. And, what is even worse, the Court has allowed this to happen, allowing notorious criminals (whose responsibility was acknowledged in statements by the prosecutors) to remain free, which discredits the judiciary and puts our country's future at risk.

Your historical responsibility is enormous. You must not allow the dismissal of any more charges...

Honorable Justices, the decision that will affirm our country's commitment to moral and ethical values is in your hands and hearts. If you negate these values, you will plunge the country into hopelessness by becoming accomplices of those who violated our nation.

FOOTNOTES

28 *The trial of the nine junta members of the "Process" lasted from April to December 1985.*

BIBLIOGRAPHY

"Closing the Book." NATION. February 28, 1987, pp.239-40.

"More Argentine Murders." CHRISTIAN CENTURY. June 8-15, 1983, p.578.

Amnesty International: *The Disappeared Of Argentina*. London, May 1979.

Amnesty International: *Report of an Amnesty International Mission to Argentina*. London, March 1977.

Amnesty International: *Testimony on Secret Detention Camps in Argentina*. London, 1979.

Amnesty International. *Torture in the Eighties: An Amnesty International Report*. 1984

Andersen, M. "Stones for Bread." NATION. May 14, 1983, p.595.

Argentina y sus derechos humanos (Asociación Patriótica Argentina), Buenos Aires, 1980.

Balderston, Daniel. *Ficción y politica: La narrativa argentina durante el proceso militar*. Alianza Editorial, 1987.

Benett, Jana and Simpson, John: *The Disappeared and the Mothers of the Plaza de Mayo*. New York: St. Martin Press, 1985.

Bousquet, Jean-Pierre: *Les folles de la place de Mai*. Stock 2, Paris, 1982.

Brown, Cynthia: *With Friends Like These: The America's Watch Report on Human Rights and U.S. Policy in Latin America*. New York: America's Watch, 1983.

Catholic Institute for International Relations: *Death and Violence in Argentina*. London, October 1976. (A report on attacks against the Roman Catholic Church and priests in Argentina.)

Chambenoix, Christian: "Buenos Aires, the Devouring Capital." *Le Monde.* Paris. 17 May 1978.

Claude, R.P. "Argentina's Return to Democracy." AMERICA. December 17, 1983, pp.385-9.

Cox, Robert J.: *The Sound of One Hand Clapping. A Preliminary Study of the Argentine Press in a Time of Terror*. Woodrow Wilson International Centre, Washington DC, August, 1980.

Crawley, Eduardo: *Argentina, a House Divided, 1880-1980*. Hurst, London, 1984.

Cunninghame Graham, Robert B.: *Tales of Horsemen*. Canongate, Edinburgh, 1981.

Di Tella, Guido: *Argentina under Perón, 1973-1976*. St. Anthony's/Macmillan Series, London, 1981.

Dougherty, M. "Unearthing a Grim Past." LIFE. May 1984, pp. 34-42.

Dworkin, Ronald. "Report from Hell," *New York Review of Books*, Volume 33, Number 12, pp.11-14.

Elon, A. "Letter from Argentina." NEW YORKER. July 21, 1986, pp.74-86.

Fisher, J. "Mothers of the Disappeared." SPARE RIB. November 1985, p.83.

Fox, E. "A Prosecution in Trouble." ATLANTIC. March 1985, p.38+.

Frasca, T. "Argentine Interlude." PROGRESSIVE. November 1984, pp.34-6.

Galeano, Eduardo: *Days and Nights of Love and War.* MONTHLY REVIEW PRESS, New York, 1983.

Girdner, W. "Torture on Trial." NATION. April 21, 1984, p.469.

Goslin, T.S. "Argentina's Desaparecidos: Investigating their Fate." CHRISTIAN CENTURY. April 17, 1985, pp.382-3.

Graham-Yooll, Andrew: *Portrait of an Exile.* Junction Books, London, 1981.

Graham-Yooll, Andrew: *A State of Fear: Memories of Argentina's Nightmare.* London, England.

Graham-Yool, Andrew: *The Press in Argentina, 1973-1978.* Writers and Scholars Educational Trust, London, 1979.

Graham-Yooll, Andrew: *The Forgotten Colony, a History of the English-Speaking Communities in Argentina.* Hutchison, London, 1981.

Griffen, A. "The Conscience of the 'Dirty War'" WOMANEWS. April, 1986, p.4.

Harvard Human Rights Yearbook. Jennifer Schirmer, "Those Who Die for Life Cannot Be Called Dead." Women and Human Rights Protest in Latin America. Volume 1, Spring 1988.

Herrera, Matilde. *José.* Buenos Aires: Editorial Contrapunto, 1987.

Hoeffel, Paul: Missing or Dead in Argentina. *THE NEW YORK TIMES MAGAZINE.* 21 May 1979.

Hopkinson, A. "Mothers Challenge Terrorism." SPARE RIB. June, 1985, p.15.

Lernoux, P. "The Threats to Argentine Democracy." NATION. February 2, 1985, p.97 + .

Mignone, Emilio F. *Iglesia y dictadura.* Buenos Aires: Ediciones del Pensamiento Nacional, 1986.

Navarro, Marysa, and Fraser, Nicholas: *Eva Perón.* André Deutsch, London, 1980.

Neier, A. "Land of Hope." NATION. December 31, 1983 - January 7, 1984, pp.684-5.

Nosiglia, Julio E. *Botín de Guerra.* Tierra Firme, 1986.

Nunca mas informe de La comisión nacional sobre la desaparición de personas Seix Barral/ Eu de BA. Buenos Aires 1985.

Organization of American States: *El Informe Prohibido Washington.* Edited by Centro de Estudios Legales, 1983.

Pally, M. "Madres: Mothers of the Plaza de Mayo." NATION. April 9, 1986, p.595.

Pérez, Juan: *Solicitada.* Edición del autor, 1986. Se obtiene al Centro de Las Madres de Plaza de Mayo, Hipolito Yrigoyén 1442 desde el año 1982.

Pingel, R. "Why the Madres Keep Marching." GUARDIAN. March 27, 1985, p.14.

Pittman, P. "Purging the Past." NATION. January 21, 1984, pp.36-7.

Pizá, Pablo: *Liliana, ¿Donde estás?.* Buenos Aires; Rafael Cedeño Editor, 1984.

Rabassa, Gregory, tr.: *The Lizard's Tale.* Farrar/Strauss Giroux, 1983.

Sábato, Ernesto, and Argentine National Commission on Disappeared People: *Nunca Más (Never Again).* Faber/Index on Censorship, London, 1986.

Seoane, María: *La Noche de los Lápices.* Buenos Aires: Editorial Contrapunto, 1986.

Soriano, Osvaldo: *No habrá más penas ni olvido.* Bruguera, Barcelona, 1980.

Stover, E. "Scientists Aid Search for Argentina's Desaparecidos." SCIENCE. October 4, 1985, pp.56-7.

Timerman, Jacobo: *Prisoner without a name, cell without a number.* Weidenfeld and Nicolson, London, 1981.

Timerman, Jacobo, tr. by Edith Grossman. "Return to Argentina." NEW YORK TIMES MAGAZINE. March 11, 1984, pp.36-40+.

Traba, Mariá: *Conversación al Sur*. México: Siglo XXI.

Traba, Marta. "Mothers in the Plaza." INDEX ON CENSOR-SHIP. March, 1986, p.5.

Valenzuela, Luisa: *Strange Things Happen Here: Twenty-Six Short Stories and a Novel*. Translated by Helen Lane. New York: H. Brace Jovanovich, 1979.

Valenzuela, L. "Making Love Visible: the Women of Buenos Aires." VOGUE. May, 1984, pp.344-5.

Vanhecke, C. "Argentina's 'Nuremberg Trial.'" WORLD PRESS REVIEW. September. 1985, pp.47-8.

Zalaquett, J. "From Dictators to Democracy." NEW REPUBLIC. December 16, 1985, pp.17-21.

In 1976, the three Epelbaum children, Luis, Claudio and Lila "disappeared". Thus began the remarkable saga of a group of women known world-wide as Madres de Plaza de Mayo — The Mothers of Plaza de Mayo.

Marjorie Agosin, author of *Scraps of Life-Chilean Arpilleras, Women of Smoke, Latin American Women in Literature* and several books of poetry. She is the recipient of many awards, among them, The New England Foundation of the Arts, Good Neighbour Award, National Association for Christian and Jews and the Distinguished Fellow Urban Morgan Institute for Human Rights, University of Cincinnati College of Law. In 1989 she received a Fullbright Scholarship. She lives in Boston with her family and teaches Spanish Literature at Wellesley College.

Renée Epelbaum was born in Parana, Argentina. An educator, music lover and businesswoman, she has travelled widely speaking out on social injustice and gaining support for the Mothers. In 1989 she received the prestigious Hadassah's *Henrietta Szold Award and Citation* in the field of Human Rights. She was also the special guest at the Bicentennial Celebration "Les Etat Generaux des Droits del'Homme" in Paris. She lives in Buenos Aires.

Janice Malloy is studying for her Ph.D in Spanish Literature, and lives in Boston.